*T*his book
belongs to

_____

*…a woman who
embraces God's grace.*

Embracing God's Grace

Elizabeth George

HARVEST HOUSE PUBLISHERS
EUGENE, OREGON

Unless otherwise indicated, all Scripture quotations are taken from the New King James Version. Copyright © 1982 by Thomas Nelson, Inc. Used by permission. All rights reserved.

Scripture quotations marked NIV are taken from the Holy Bible, New International Version®, NIV®. Copyright © 1973, 1978, 1984 by Biblica, Inc.™ Used by permission of Zondervan. All rights reserved worldwide.

Harvest House Publishers, Inc. is the exclusive licensee of the trademark A WOMAN AFTER GOD'S OWN HEART.

Cover by Dugan Design Group, Bloomington, Minnesota

Cover photo © Thomas Dobner 2008 / Alamy

Back cover photo © Harry Langdon

Acknowledgments

As always, thank you to my dear husband, Jim George, MDiv, ThM, for your able assistance, guidance, suggestions, and loving encouragement on this project.

A very special thank you to Steve Miller, senior editor at Harvest House Publishers, for your help and direction in making this study a reality.

EMBRACING GOD'S GRACE
Copyright © 2010 by Elizabeth George
Published by Harvest House Publishers
Eugene, Oregon 97402
www.harvesthousepublishers.com

ISBN 978-0-7369-1246-4 (pbk.)
ISBN 978-0-7369-3571-5 (eBook)

Printed in the United States of America

15   16   / BP-NI /   10   9   8   7   6   5   4

Contents

Foreword

Before You Begin

Foreword

For some time I have been looking for Bible studies that I could use each day that would increase my knowledge of God's Word. In my search, I found myself struggling between two extremes: Bible studies that required little time but also had little substance, or studies that were in-depth and demanded more time than I could give. I discovered that I wasn't alone—there were many other women like me who were busy yet desired to spend quality time studying God's Word.

That's why I became excited when Elizabeth George shared her desire to create a series of women's Bible studies that offered in-depth lessons that could be completed in just 15-20 minutes per day. When she completed the first study—on Philippians—I was eager to try it out. I had already studied Philippians many times, but this was the first time I had come to understand exactly how the whole book fit together and how it can truly be lived out in my life. Each lesson was simple but insightful—and was written especially to apply to me as a woman!

In the Woman After God's Own Heart® Bible study series, Elizabeth takes you step by step through the Scriptures, sharing wisdom she has gleaned from more than 20 years as a women's Bible teacher. The lessons are rich and meaningful because they're rooted in God's Word and have been lived out in Elizabeth's life. Her thoughtful and personable guidance makes you feel as though you are studying right alongside her—as if she is personally mentoring you in the greatest aspiration you could ever pursue: to become a woman after God's own heart.

If you're looking for Bible studies that can help you grow stronger in your knowledge of God's Word even in the most demanding of schedules, I know you'll find this series to be a welcome companion in your daily walk with God.

—LaRae Weikert
Vice President of Editorial,
Harvest House Publishers

Before You Begin

In my book *A Woman After God's Own Heart*®, I describe such a woman as one who ensures that God is first in her heart and the Ultimate Priority of her life. Then I share that one crucial way this desire can become reality is by nurturing a heart that abides in God's Word. To do so means that you and I must develop a root system anchored deep in God's Word.

Before you launch into this Bible study, take a moment to think about these aspects of a root system produced by the regular, faithful study of God's Word:

- *Roots are unseen*—You'll want to set aside time in solitude— "underground" if you will—to immerse yourself in God's Word and grow in Him.

- *Roots are for taking in*—Alone and with your Bible in hand, you'll want to take in and feed upon the truths of the Word of God and ensure your spiritual growth.

- *Roots are for storage*—As you form the habit of looking into God's Word, you'll find a vast, deep reservoir of divine hope and strength forming for the rough times.

- *Roots are for support*—Do you want to stand strong in the Lord? To stand firm against the pressures of life? The routine care of your roots through exposure to God's Word will cultivate you into a remarkable woman of endurance.*

I'm glad you've chosen this study out of my A Woman After God's Own Heart® Bible study series. My prayer for you is that the truths you find in God's Word through this study will further transform your life into the image of His dear Son and empower you to be the woman you seek to be: a woman after God's own heart.

In His love,

Elizabeth George

---

* Taken from Elizabeth George, *A Woman After God's Own Heart* (Eugene, OR: Harvest House Publishers, 2006), pp. 31-36.

hether you lived 2000 years ago or you're alive today, God's message is the same—His grace is total and complete. Nothing needs to be added. As you study verse by verse through Colossians and Philemon you'll realize the sufficiency of Christ more deeply as you discover...

- God's grace offered through the ministry of others

- God's grace manifested in the life and ministry of Christ

- God's grace exhibited in a Christian home

- God's grace shown in the workplace

- God's grace witnessed in the forgiveness of others

This uplifting study will give you a more thorough understanding of the person and work of Jesus Christ. You'll be encouraged as you see firsthand how His life is lived out in practical and exciting ways through ordinary people.

Greeting the Brethren

Colossians 1:1-2

When you're a published author, it's assumed that you know something about writing. That's one reason I'm often asked to read, give suggestions for, and endorse book manuscripts. However, because of my packed schedule and limited time, I have to graciously decline. But on occasion, if I personally know the author of a book, I will agree to write an endorsement of the person and their ministry. This endorsement lets people know what I admire and appreciate about the author of the work.

As we begin our study of the New Testament epistle of Colossians, that's exactly what the great apostle Paul is doing. He's writing his endorsement of a group of believers—a church body—he's never met, yet whose spiritual qualities he's heard a great deal about. In addition, Paul is sending an endorsement to the church of the very man who has brought him a glowing report of the growing and dynamic Christians

11

in Colosse. But as Paul's letter progresses, he also voices concerns for their continued spiritual growth.

Let's now look at what Paul, a powerful encourager, has to say about embracing God's grace.

Colossians 1:1-2

1 Paul, an apostle of Jesus Christ by the will of God, and Timothy our brother,

2 To the saints and faithful brethren in Christ who are in Colosse: Grace to you and peace from God our Father and the Lord Jesus Christ.

Out of God's Word...

1. *Paul*—How does Paul describe himself in verse 1?

Using an English dictionary, define an *apostle*.

How does Paul say he became an apostle?

What additional information do these scriptures tell you about Paul?

Romans 1:1—

Galatians 1:1—

What else do you learn about Paul's situation in Colossians 4:3?

2. *Paul's companion*—What other person is mentioned in this greeting to the Colossians (verse 1)?

What do we know about him from these verses?

Acts 16:1-3—

Philippians 2:19-22—

2 Timothy 1:5—

2 Timothy 3:15—

3. *Paul's readers*—How does Paul describe those who will read his letter (verse 2)?

Where are his readers located?

The city of Colosse was 100 miles east of Ephesus on the Lycus River and included what was known as the "Asian region." Colosse was not as influential as the nearby city of Laodicea, but as a trading center and crossroads, it exerted an impact on religious thinking and philosophy.

What do you learn about Paul's ministry in Ephesus as he speaks to the Ephesian elders in Acts 20:31?

How widely did the message spread beyond Ephesus according to Acts 19:10?

4. *Paul's greeting*—What two greetings does Paul offer to his readers in verse 2?

—

—

What is the source of these blessings (verse 2)?

...*and into Your Heart*

• *Your role as a mentor/discipler*—Paul's mention of Timothy brings to mind the issue of mentoring or discipleship. More than 10 years have passed since Paul first asked young Timothy to join his missionary team. Timothy has been nurtured and trained to the point he is now a seasoned missionary. So much so that he is capable of passing on to others what he learned from Paul so they too can grow spiritually. Titus 2:3-5 describes the role "older women" are to play in this mentoring and training process. Who does God say your students are (verse 4)?

What are you to teach them (verses 4-5)?

—

—

—

—

—

—

—

What does Paul say you should do to prepare yourself for fulfilling this role (verse 3)?

How important is it to mentor and disciple young women?

What part can you play in training up the next generation of godly women?

Can you think of any areas in which you need preparation so you can teach others?

- *Your position and practice*—Paul referred to the Colossian Christians as "saints" or "set apart ones." You, along with them, are not a saint because of any merit of your own. You are a saint because you have been set apart by God's great grace to devote yourself to a holy and pure way of life. This is your fixed spiritual *position* in Christ.

But how are you doing when it comes to living in the real world of practical everyday life? What qualities in your life and actions would cause you and others to describe you as "faithful"? List a few here, then any areas that need improvement. Make it your goal to leave no room for doubt about your faithfulness to Christ.

- *Your blessings*—Paul offers two blessings to the Colossians in his greeting. Both have as their source "God our Father and the Lord Jesus Christ." "Grace" means God's unmerited favor. And "peace" is what Jesus established between believers and the Father through His death on the cross. With God as your Father, you now have "peace from God" and the "peace" of God. Read Ephesians 2:8 and comment on God's grace in your life.

Heart Response

Paul had a deep love for Jesus Christ, and that love spilled out of his heart and into the letters of love and concern he wrote to the people in various churches, including the church at Colosse. His heart was always burdened for churches everywhere. He was devoted to encouraging and correcting believers regarding anything that was happening to them or might happen.

Now, the church in Colosse was not situated in an important city. It was more like a small-town church. Why, who in the world would care about them?!

Well, Paul cared! And he was thrilled by their growth and maturity. However, when he heard about a serious doctrinal error in the church at Colosse, he was compelled—out of love and a caring heart—to write this letter.

Consider your love for Jesus. As you begin this study and continue to read and live the truths in the book of Colossians, think about these things: First, how is your spiritual growth? What does your growth curve look like? Next, do you know any believers you could help to better understand God's grace and the Christian faith? Be sure to pray for them. Also ask God to show you how you can assist them with a heart of love. And finally, in what ways can you share what you're learning with those around you—your family, friends, and coworkers? With those who don't know Jesus?

Follow Paul's example and do what you can. Pray for those you know. Encourage others. Make it your heart's intent to let them know about God's truly amazing grace!

Giving Thanks to God

Colossians 1:3-8

A forgiven sinner is a thankful saint. This statement typifies the life and ministry of the great apostle Paul. You may already know that Paul, formerly a Pharisee, was a vicious persecutor of Christians in the newly born church. But Paul, also known as Saul, was gloriously transformed when he was on his way to Damascus to arrest even more Christians. It's no wonder offerings of thanks to God showed up often in this forgiven sinner's writings. And his letter to the believers in Colosse is no exception. Paul not only gives thanks to God and his Savior, the Lord Jesus Christ, but he also gives thanks for the spiritual growth of those in the Colossian church. Follow along and discover what it means to look beyond yourself and your situation and be thankful for all that God is doing in the world around you.

Colossians 1:3-8

³ We give thanks to the God and Father of our Lord Jesus Christ, praying always for you,

⁴ since we heard of your faith in Christ Jesus and of your love for all the saints;

⁵ because of the hope which is laid up for you in heaven, of which you heard before in the word of the truth of the gospel,

⁶ which has come to you, as it has also in all the world, and is bringing forth fruit, as it is also among you since the day you heard and knew the grace of God in truth;

⁷ as you also learned from Epaphras, our dear fellow servant, who is a faithful minister of Christ on your behalf,

⁸ who also declared to us your love in the Spirit.

Out of God's Word...

1. *The primary focus of thanksgiving*—Paul begins his letter to his readers by giving thanks to whom (verse 3)?

2. *The reasons for thanksgiving*—As you read through verses 4-6, look for the many reasons Paul had for giving thanks for what was happening in the lives of the Colossian believers. Take a look at them now, as follows:

Verse 4—Note the things Paul heard about the Colossians that moved him to thank God.

—

—

Verse 5—Add yet another reason Paul had for giving thanks to God.

Verses 5-6—Next Paul turns to "the word of the truth of the gospel." What effect was it having on the readers?

Verses 7-8—Paul also gives thanks for a person. Who was he, and how does Paul describe him and his ministry?

...and into Your Heart

- *Giving thanks in prayer*—Paul had developed the habit of prayer. What does Ephesians 6:18 say about prayer?

And what does Ephesians 6:18 say about the scope of prayer?

Note the message from each of these verses about the habit and practice of prayer:

Luke 18:1—

Philippians 4:6—

Colossians 4:2—

1 Thessalonians 5:17—

A habit is a repeated act and can be good or bad. List several things you can do and changes you can make right away—today!—to develop the better habit of prayer—genuine, regular, faithful, continuous prayer.

* *Giving thanks to God*—Paul is thankful for the Colossians' response to the truth of God's Word. At the same time, he's aware that honor and glory are due to God alone for all he has heard and witnessed of the believers' growth. Paul's commendation of the growth and fruit in the saints in Colosse is transformed into a prayer of thanksgiving to God, the One who is ultimately responsible for the spiritual advancement of His children. Read Ephesians 3:8-9 and then try your hand at writing out your own prayer of thanks to God for your salvation.

Bonus question: Read another of Paul's prayers, which appears in Philippians 1:9-11. This is a prayer for the spiritual growth of those he loved. List what Paul prayed for his friends:

Verse 9—

Verse 10—

Verse 11—

Who needs your prayers for spiritual growth? Your child? Grandchild? Nieces, nephews, and cousins? Your husband or parents? A daughter- or son-in-law? List several names below. Then begin now to pray as Paul did. Use his words, if you like. Lift your prayers to God on their behalf. And when you see evidence of spiritual fruit, don't forget to give thanks to God as Paul did.

* *Giving thanks for growth*—Spiritual growth seems to come with struggles. Somehow it always seems we take two steps forward and one back! Maybe that's one reason we're so thankful to God when we see growth in ourself and in other believers. Paul was incredibly thankful to hear about the spiritual growth in the Colossians— a steadfast *faith* in Jesus and a *love* that went beyond an inner circle to include all. All their growth was motivated by the assurance of a future *hope* of eternity with their Savior. How do you rate your spiritual growth? Point to

a few specific areas in which you've seen change and improvement.

Now think of several people you know whose growth has been obvious. What changes have you noticed? Give thanks to God...and don't forget to mention your observations to these people. As Proverbs 12:25 says, a good word makes the heart glad. Everyone can use a word of encouragement!

• *Giving thanks for faithful ministers*—Paul was also thankful for the faithful ministry of Epaphras, who was commissioned by Paul to take the gospel to Colosse. Epaphras was "a faithful minister of Christ" (Colossians 1:7) on behalf of the Colossians.

   Ministers of Christ labor on our behalf. How faithful are you to pray for your pastor, church leaders, Bible teachers, missionaries, and mentors? List several people who labor for God and for the good of others. Give thanks to God for those people...and think of some ways you can show your appreciation for their faithful labor of love.

Heart Response

Unfortunately, you and I live in a very negative world. If we're not careful that negative spirit can rub off on us. It's all too easy to become as cynical as the next person. But Paul wasn't about to let his surroundings rub off on him. Even though he was under house arrest in Rome, where he was writing to the Colossians, Paul opened his letter with pure thanksgiving. His heart was filled and overflowing with "faith in Christ Jesus" and a "love for all the saints." He blessed God. Then blessed God for what He was doing in the lives of others. And finally, he blessed God for using others to take the gospel to the ends of the earth. What's not to be thankful for?!

And the same holds true for you. Look to God. Open your eyes. Look for evidence of His grace. Behold what He is doing in the world and in the lives of others. When you do, it won't be long before you stop worrying about your problems and start praising God for His magnificent power...and for "the hope which is laid up for you in heaven."

Praying for Spiritual Maturity

Colossians 1:9-12

*M*otherhood is a unique and honored privilege and should never be taken for granted. A mother's duties start early...and end late. A good mom is always vigilant, always watching, and always warning. She desires that her children grow up and became physically healthy adults. But a *Christian* mom has an even greater concern—she cares passionately for her children's spiritual growth.

Paul is very much like a Christian mother. Even though he has never met the believers in Colosse, he is fiercely concerned for their spiritual growth and maturity (2:1). He rejoices in the news of their growth so far. Yet because there's always room for increased spiritual maturity, he prays for even greater growth. He prays especially that they would gain greater knowledge of God, His grace, and His will for them. Sit quietly beside Paul in his prison cell and learn how to pray for the spiritual maturity of others. Listen to his prayer...and his heart.

Colossians 1:9-12

⁹ For this reason we also, since the day we heard it,
do not cease to pray for you, and to ask that you
may be filled with the knowledge of His will in all
wisdom and spiritual understanding;

¹⁰ that you may walk worthy of the Lord, fully
pleasing Him, being fruitful in every good work
and increasing in the knowledge of God;

¹¹ strengthened with all might, according to His glo-
rious power, for all patience and longsuffering with
joy;

¹² giving thanks to the Father who has qualified us to
be partakers of the inheritance of the saints in the
light.

Out of God's Word...

1. Even though Paul was more than 1000 miles away from
the Colossian believers, what ministry did he have in their
lives (verse 9)?

2. What was the first request Paul lifted up to God for the
Colossians (verse 9)?

What is essential in knowing God's will?

—

—

3. When you obey God, you show evidence of true knowledge and understanding of His will. What is the result of a clear knowledge of God's will (verse 10)?

List the three activities of one who pleases Him.

   Verse 10—

   Verse 10—

   Verse 11—

Where does this strength come from?

What qualities does this strength give?

   —

   —

   —

Paul's expression of thanksgiving extends over the next three verses (12-14). What does he give thanks for in verse 12?

...and into Your Heart

- *Paul's prayer life*—Paul's 13 letters contain a generous sprinkling of his prayers for his readers. A number of his letters were written while in prison. Chances are that Paul's confinement in prison provided him with lots of time to pray. But even when Paul was busily engaged in ministry while in Corinth, he made time to write to the Thessalonians, letting them know he was constantly remembering them in his prayers (1 Thessalonians 1:3).

  We often use busyness as an excuse for not praying. But as paraphrased from Martin Luther, "My schedule is so busy today, I needed to spend more time in prayer." Don't let a busy life keep you from prayer. You need it! And, like the Colossians, others need your prayers for their maturity as well. Comment on this statement: Maybe the reason my life is so busy and often out of control is because I don't stop and pray for God's priorities in my life.

- *Paul's prayers*—Have you ever attended a prayer meeting in which most of the prayers were about people's physical needs? I know I have. Well, if Paul's prayers are to serve as models that teach us how to pray, we just might discover we're praying with the wrong emphasis! What did Paul focus on in some of his prayers?

  Ephesians 1:15-19—

  Ephesians 3:14-19—

  1 Thessalonians 1:2-4—

Praying for physical needs is not wrong. However, like Paul, you need to pray for the spiritual maturity of other believers, starting with your own family. Make a list of family members and then jot down some spiritual concerns you could begin to pray for using some elements of Paul's prayer here in verses 9-12 as your guide.

* *Paul's thankfulness*—Before becoming a Christian, Paul would have only been "qualified" to receive God's wrath. But by the grace of God through Jesus Christ, Paul was "made sufficient," "authorized" to receive an inheritance. He rejoiced in this, and you perhaps noticed he wanted to include others in his thanksgiving.

  Have you received Jesus Christ into your life as your Savior? Then you too have an inheritance. You too can give abundant, heartfelt thanks! To better appreciate your inheritance, look ahead at 1:13 and describe the brief information given about that inheritance.

What additional information about your inheritance can you gain from reading Ephesians 1:11-14?

And 1 Peter 1:3-5?

Your inheritance exists in the spiritual realm where God Himself dwells, the place of divine illumination—the place of light, God's kingdom. Write a short prayer of thanksgiving for your spiritual inheritance.

Heart Response

Do you ever wonder how to pray for people you've never met? They may be missionaries, spiritual leaders, or even people you don't know in your own church. Paul had never met the Colossians, but he faithfully prayed for them and their spiritual maturity. When you don't know how to pray for others, follow the example Paul set in his prayers for the Colossians.

- Pray that they understand God's will.

- Pray that they gain spiritual wisdom.

- Pray that they please God in every area of life.

- Pray that they bear fruit.

- Pray that they grow in their knowledge of God.

- Pray that they be filled with God's strength so they can patiently endure whatever comes their way.

- Pray that they rejoice and always give thanks.

- Pray that they grow in grace.

Prayer is a mighty ministry that any believer can have—anywhere, anytime, and in any circumstance. When Paul was confined, he prayed. When he was free and on the move, he prayed. And his prayers were constant! To the Christians in Thessalonica he said, "We give thanks to God *always* for you all, making mention of you in our prayers."

Don't neglect the important area of prayer in your Christian life. Accept the challenge. Make it a priority. You may be the only one praying for another person. And don't forget to focus your prayers on spiritual concerns. The spiritual condition of that person will determine how well she is able to cope with life's issues, whether those issues are physical or emotional.

esson 4

Grasping the Preeminence of Christ

Colossians 1:13-18

*H*e is risen" (Matthew 28:6) is the declaration made by the angel at Jesus' empty tomb. The resurrection of Jesus is at the heart and soul of Christianity. It is the "good news"! It is the message that Peter offered on the Day of Pentecost (Acts 2:32), and 3000 people believed and were baptized. It was the reality that Paul faced as he met the risen Lord on the Damascus Road (Acts 9). The resurrection was the central theme of Paul's message from that time onward, and he resounded that theme in his letter to the Colossian church. The resurrection of Jesus and His offer of redemption was possible only if Jesus was God. And here in Colossians 1:13-18, Paul reminds the Colossian believers of the preeminence of Christ, and what He did to bring about their redemption. Follow along as Paul asks the Colossians to try and comprehend the amazing grace of God, the Father, in sending His Son, the Lord Jesus Christ, to be their Redeemer.

Colossians 1:13-18

¹³ He has delivered us from the power of darkness and conveyed us into the kingdom of the Son of His love,

¹⁴ in whom we have redemption through His blood, the forgiveness of sins.

¹⁵ He is the image of the invisible God, the firstborn over all creation.

¹⁶ For by Him all things were created that are in heaven and that are on earth, visible and invisible, whether thrones or dominions or principalities or powers. All things were created through Him and for Him.

¹⁷ And He is before all things, and in Him all things consist.

¹⁸ And He is the head of the body, the church, who is the beginning, the firstborn from the dead, that in all things He may have the preeminence.

Out of God's Word...

1. *The Father's role*—What part did God the Father play in our redemption (verse 13)?

    —

    —

2. *The Son's role*—What made our redemption possible (verse 14)?

   What is the benefit of this redemption (verse 14)?

3. *The Son's identity*—List Paul's description of the Person of Christ.

   Verse 15—

   Verse 15—

   Verse 17—

   Verse 17—

   Verse 18—

   Verse 18—

   Verse 18—

4. *The Son's work*—List the extent of Christ's work in creation (verse 16).

...and into Your Heart

The Colossians had been rescued by God from vile pagan beliefs and practices. The report of their spiritual growth had encouraged Paul. Their faith, love, and hope were evident. They were bearing fruit. Yet there was always the danger they would slip back into their former habits—especially if they forgot about their past.

- *Their redemption*—Paul's expressions of thanksgiving that began in verse 12 extend through verse 18. One major area of thanksgiving involves our redemption. The Father "qualified" us and by His greater power "delivered" us from the power of darkness and placed us into the kingdom of His Son. What does Ephesians 1:7 say about the extent or source of our redemption and forgiveness?

  Reflect back on your past before God's grace was offered to you in Jesus. You have many reasons to be thankful, don't you? Write out a line or two of your own prayer of thanksgiving!

- *Their Savior*—Paul heard that false teaching had filtered into the church at Colosse. The specific heresy is not stated, but it seems to try to diminish the person and work of Christ. Paul explains in no uncertain terms that the Colossian believers must recognize the deity of Jesus Christ and His work on their behalf. Jesus is God, and their faith requires that He have and hold this exalted position of Creator, Sustainer, and Savior. Here are a few key phrases that describe the supremacy of Christ—only a Person with these qualifications could qualify to be their Savior:

Image of the invisible God—Jesus is the exact visible representation of God. He is in the very form of God and has been so from all eternity (verse 15).

The firstborn over all creation—This doesn't mean Jesus was the first to be created, for He is eternal. That He is the firstborn means He is first in rank. Jesus has the priority and authority of the firstborn of a king's household. Therefore, He is supreme over all creation, including the spirit world.

He is the Creator—Jesus is God in human flesh. His name *Immanuel* literally means "God with us" (Matthew 1:23). So He was present at creation and all things were created "through Him and for Him" (Colossians 1:16).

He is the head of the body—Christ controls every part of the church and gives it life and direction. As the first to be resurrected, Christ is supreme over all who will ever be raised from the dead and that includes all people, both believers and unbelievers (verse 18).

How should Christ's preeminence affect your response to Him in even the smallest areas of your life?

Heart Response

Jesus is eternally supreme. He is supreme in all respects, and at every point. He is Lord of creation, and Lord of His church. Therefore He must be Lord of His own. Are you one of His children? If so, He expects no rivals in your life. He expects...

> your worship, praise, and thanks,
>
> your willingness to learn more about Him and His grace,
>
> your wholehearted devotion to Him, and
>
> your heartfelt love for what He has done for you.

Are there areas of your life that you are attempting to withhold from Christ's authority? Can you pinpoint them? Name them? Take a moment to surrender those areas to Him now.

If you are not a child of God, why not relinquish control of your life right now and experience God's transforming grace? Your prayer might go something like this:

> God, I want to yield control of my life to You. I want to turn away from sin and receive Your Son, Jesus Christ, as my Lord and Savior. Thank You for sending Him to the cross to die for me and pay for my sins so that I might have His righteousness. I give my life to You now, asking that You would guide me. Thank You for the grace You have shown to me!

# Lesson 5

Realizing What Christ Has Done for You

Colossians 1:19-23

've told you a hundred times not to do that!" Did your parents ever say that to you? Or have you ever made an exaggerated comment like this to one of your children? In reality, maybe it was only a few times you scolded your little darling. So why did you overstate your case? For effect. Right? Well, you are not alone. The apostle Paul did the same when he wrote to a group of believers in a small backwater town in Asia Minor. Paul used hyperbole, or a bit of exaggeration, to get his point across. He wanted his readers to have no mistake about who Jesus is and what He has graciously done for them. Follow along and see if you can pick up Paul's use of hyperbole as you read this passage.

Colossians 1:19-23

¹⁹ For it pleased the Father that in Him all the fullness should dwell,

²⁰ and by Him to reconcile all things to Himself, by Him, whether things on earth or things in heaven, having made peace through the blood of His cross.

²¹ And you, who once were alienated and enemies in your mind by wicked works, yet now He has reconciled

²² in the body of His flesh through death, to present you holy, and blameless, and above reproach in His sight—

²³ if indeed you continue in the faith, grounded and steadfast, and are not moved away from the hope of the gospel which you heard, which was preached to every creature under heaven, of which I, Paul, became a minister.

Out of God's Word...

The word "for" in verse 19 points to what has just been stated by Paul in verses 15-18. Christ is supreme. His supremacy proceeds from the fact that the incarnate Son is fully divine and that this unique divine-human person is the visible expression of the pleasure of the Father.

1. Because Jesus is the dwelling place of the fullness of God He is able to...

...do what (verse 20)?

To what extent (verse 20)?

How (verse 20)?

2. What was your twofold condition before Christ's intervention (verse 21)?

—

—

3. What is the threefold result of His intervention (verse 22)?

—

—

—

4. What cautions does Paul use (verse 23)?

—

—

—

—

...and into Your Heart

Before the sacrificial death of Christ on the cross, sinners like you and me were alienated from a holy God. But with Christ's death and resurrection, it is possible, by faith, to be reconciled to God. Reconciliation is a central theme of the gospel message.

- *Your former condition*—As with all of Paul's writings, there is an intensely personal application to his readers starting in verse 21. He wants them to remember their past.

  How was this inner attitude demonstrated?

  Where had this rebellion left them?

  Reflect again on your past, your life before you had a relationship with Christ. For what are you thankful?

- *Your future condition*—Transformation has its beginning at salvation. The process has begun and will continue until you arrive in glory. Here's what the future holds for the Colossians:

  Holy—The ultimate aim of their reconciliation is that God present them before Himself in holiness—a state of separation from sin.

Blameless—Christ desires to present them spotless, with a purity that has its source in Himself, "a lamb...without spot" (1 Peter 1:19).

Above reproach—No accusation may be laid against them (Romans 8:33).

As I said earlier, the process has started. How would you evaluate your present progress...

...in separation from sin?

...in purity?

...in conduct?

Give thanks for your growth, and make plans to do something about areas that need improvement.

- *Your present faithfulness*—God has ordained the believers' ultimate end (verse 22), and He's also ordained the means to that end, their continuing faithfulness (verse 23). Divine *preservation* always presupposes human *perseverance*. Paul assumes that his readers will continue in their faith. He is like a coach standing on the sideline and encouraging his team, the Colossians—and you!—to remain faithful even in the midst of temptation and false teaching. How are you doing? Are you faltering in any area of your life? What do you think Coach

Paul would tell you to do? Jot down an area of your life in which you are faltering.

• *The scope of the gospel*—Paul called himself a "minister" or servant of the gospel (verse 23). This is the same term he used to describe Epaphras in 1:7. He wanted his readers to know they were not alone in their beliefs. He wanted them to know that, unlike the false teaching that had come into their midst, which was secretive and limited to a few "enlightened" ones, the gospel that his readers had heard and responded to was spreading and was available to the whole world! There was no excuse for wandering away into false teaching. Write Romans 1:16 below, then state your commitment to the gospel of Christ.

Heart Response

Christ's death opened the door for all people—including you—to come to God. It took away the sin that keeps you from having a right relationship with God. The way has been cleared. You can have peace with God. If you have accepted Christ, who died in your place, you are among those who are saved. If you haven't done this, don't wait until it's too late. Be reconciled to God. Come to Him by grace through Christ.

Lesson 6

Serving Christ Sacrificially

Colossians 1:24-26

Most people try to avoid sacrifice and pain if they can. But from the moment sin entered the world, pain and suffering were the consequences. I have by no means suffered like many of my friends and acquaintances. As I write this lesson, several family members are suffering physically, and my oldest brother died recently. And I am not alone. I'm sure you could make your own list as well. No, we don't enjoy pain and suffering, and we certainly don't go out of our way to find it. But in Colossians 1:24-26, Paul says he actually rejoices in his suffering and that he looks forward to even more suffering as he serves his Master, Jesus. Wow! What an attitude! What possesses him to make such unusual statements? Follow along to learn the secrets to sacrificial service.

Colossians 1:24-26

²⁴ I now rejoice in my sufferings for you, and fill up in my flesh what is lacking in the afflictions of Christ, for the sake of His body, which is the church,

²⁵ of which I became a minister according to the stewardship from God which was given to me for you, to fulfill the word of God,

²⁶ the mystery which has been hidden from ages and from generations, but now has been revealed to His saints.

Out of God's Word...

The word "now" speaks of what Paul was talking about in verses 21-23. There we learned about Christ's reconciliation of His own, the formation of His body, the church, and Paul's present condition of imprisonment.

1. What two things does Paul say he is prepared to do for God's people, particularly the Colossians (verse 24)?

    —

    —

    For whose sake is he willing to suffer?

2. What is Paul's perspective on his call to the ministry (verse 25)?

—

—

3. How does Paul describe what he calls "the mystery" (verse 26)?

—

—

...and into Your Heart

Paul is not complaining about his suffering. No, he rejoices. Paul sees suffering on behalf of Christ as a great privilege. His example should serve to strengthen the Colossians and believers everywhere in their faith. Paul's suffering gives him every right to talk of his sufferings for them. So let's look at suffering.

- *Jesus' view of suffering*—By identifying themselves with Christ, all believers will face affliction. What was Jesus' initial comment on suffering in John 15:20-21?

   What can we learn about the apostles and suffering for Jesus in these verses?

Acts 5:41—

Acts 9:16—

Romans 8:17—

How should you view suffering?

2 Corinthians 1:6-7—

2 Corinthians 4:7-12—

James 1:2—

1 Peter 1:6-7—

After looking at these different verses on suffering, how should you approach...

...suffering for Jesus' sake?

...suffering physically?

• *Lacking in the afflictions of Christ*—This does not mean there was anything lacking in the atoning value of Christ's sacrifice. Nor does it mean that you or I can add to the merits of our Lord's sacrifice. His sacrifice was perfect and complete. What it does mean is that as members of Christ's body, the church, we, along with Paul, share the suffering that Christ endured during His earthly ministry, and which we now continue to endure as an extension of Him. Reflect again on the question of suffering for Jesus' sake. Do you need to add anything to your answer?

Heart Response

The apostle Paul saw his suffering as part of God's divine purpose. He gladly accepted it as doing his part in fulfilling the grand plan of God. Do you view suffering in the same broader context, or do you see your suffering as affecting only you and upsetting your plans? When you suffer, do you find yourself complaining, "Why me?"

Yes, suffering is painful. We certainly prefer not to go through it. But if you are now enduring suffering, or when you do encounter it, ask God to give you the grace to see the bigger picture, to have an eternal perspective. Ask Him for the grace to "count it all joy" (James 1:2) when suffering comes your way. Rejoice! God is at work, and you get to take part in His grand and marvelous plan. Be faithful while you suffer—knowing that you, along with all the saints, have the crown of life waiting for you (Revelation 2:10)!

*L*esson 7

Understanding
the Mystery

I don't know about you, but I enjoy a good mystery. My fascination for mystery stories started as a young girl with the Nancy Drew mystery series. I devoured those books—each story left me sitting on the edge of my chair as I followed Nancy as she pursued the clues that eventually solved another mystery.

The apostle Paul, like Nancy Drew, is about to solve a mystery. He first mentions the "mystery" in Colossians 1:26 when he cryptically says this secret had been hidden for a long time—in fact, thousands of years. Follow along as Paul unfolds this secret.

Colossians 1:27-29

²⁷ To them God willed to make known what are the riches of the glory of this mystery among the Gentiles: which is Christ in you, the hope of glory.

²⁸ Him we preach, warning every man and teaching every man in all wisdom, that we may present every man perfect in Christ Jesus.

²⁹ To this end I also labor, striving according to His working which works in me mightily.

Out of God's Word...

1. Read again verse 26 as Paul begins to reveal what he calls "the mystery." Who is Paul speaking about when he uses the word "them" in verse 27?

2. What are the elements of this mystery as described in verse 27?

    Its value—

    Its recipients—

    Its meaning—

    Its result—

3. After explaining that Christ is the center of the mystery, Paul continues in verse 28. What are the elements of this preaching to "every man"?

   —

   —

   —

4. Describe what is involved for Paul or anyone who fulfills this great task of maturing the saints (verse 29).

   —

   —

   —

...and into Your Heart

- *Your understanding of the mystery*—You, like the Colossian believers, might be a little mystified about this mystery Paul mentions. He doesn't say much. But it wouldn't be long before the Colossians would receive more details. In Colossians 4:16, Paul tells his readers about a letter he is sending to the town of Laodicea. Bible scholars believe this letter to be the book of Ephesians, which would then be sent to Colosse to be read. The believers in Ephesus would receive a more detailed description of what this mystery was all about when they read "the epistle from Laodicea" (4:16). Scan Ephesians chapter 3 to see what Paul says about this mystery.

How did Paul receive this mystery (verse 3)?

Who revealed this mystery, and who was it revealed to (verse 5)?

How does Paul describe this mystery (verse 6)?

• *Your relationship with Christ*—The idea that the Messiah would dwell among His people, the Jews, was well documented in the Old Testament. But what was shrouded in mystery was that *the Messiah of Israel would also dwell among the Gentiles.* This was an entirely new revelation of the purposes of God. The majority of churches around Ephesus, including the churches at Laodicea and Colosse, were made up mostly of Gentiles. So this was good news to them as believers.

If you are a believer, Christ indwells you. That's the mystery! Do you have what Paul calls God's pledge of "the hope of glory" (verse 27)? Briefly describe your personal relationship with Christ.

• *Your responsibility to Christ*—Christ is here described as the center of God's message to the world. This message comes in three phases:

Warning—to admonish, to encourage, to stimulate, to plead. Paul was not cold and indifferent in his preaching.

How did Paul show his emotions while he ministered in Ephesus (Acts 20:19)?

In Corinth (2 Corinthians 2:4)?

In Philippi (Philippians 3:18)?

Make a brief list of the heart attitudes you experience as you consider sharing God's truth with others. Do any of these need to go? What better attitudes should take their place?

Teaching—Christianity is based on knowledge, on doctrine. Doctrine is communicated through teaching, and the qualifier is that teaching be done in "all wisdom," which comes from God. Teaching can be formal, as in a classroom or at a Bible study. Or it can be informal, in everyday life situations. Has God gifted you to teach His Word in a classroom or at a Bible study? If so, what are you—or should you be—doing to use and improve this gift?

Not everyone is gifted for the formal teaching of God's truths and the gospel. But every believer teaches others informally through his or her life. How does Paul describe the way the Corinthians taught informally through their lives in 2 Corinthians 3:3?

Note a few ways you are currently teaching through your life to your family.

To your neighbors.

To your fellow members at church.

Discipleship—The goal of mentoring is to nurture others toward spiritual maturity, or, as Paul said, "present every man perfect in Christ." How does Paul describe this process in the following verses?

Acts 20:27 (the Ephesian elders)—

Philippians 4:9—

Titus 2:3-5—

What additional steps could you take to further disciple and mentor any children still at home?

Are you actively mentoring other women? What can you do to be more involved in this vital ministry?

Heart Response

The mystery is solved! If Christ is your Savior, you have His Spirit living in you and you have the "hope of glory." There is coming a day when you will be present with Christ, at home in glory! But until then, you have a big responsibility. You are to teach and disciple. As I said earlier, this doesn't mean you must do this formally and stand on a street corner and preach the gospel or teach a Bible study. What it does mean is that your life may be the only Bible that many people will ever read. Make sure others—starting with your family—are able to look at your life example and get an accurate picture of Jesus and His grace and power to transform lives!

Lesson 8

Encouraging Growth in Believers

I'm sure you have felt concern for the welfare of another person. Who hasn't? Maybe it's for a husband fighting a war in a far-off land. Or a child fighting another kind of war in a faraway college. For the one it's a particular concern for physical safety. For the other it's not only physical safety, but also spiritual stability as the child faces the world in all its fury. Well, Paul too has some concerns as he writes to a group of people in the small town of Colosse, despite the fact he's never met them face-to-face.

So what do you do when you have a concern for someone far away? Obviously prayer is a starting point. What's next? You can write a letter and offer encouragement. Paul has been doing just that. First he tells the Colossians he prays continuously for them (1:9). Then he lets them know of his specific "conflicts" regarding their growth. Follow along as Paul shows us how a word of praise makes a word of concern, warning, or re-buke much easier to accept.

Colossians 2:1-10

1 For I want you to know what a great conflict I have for you and those in Laodicea, and for as many as have not seen my face in the flesh,

2 that their hearts may be encouraged, being knit together in love, and *attaining* to all riches of the full assurance of understanding, to the knowledge of the mystery of God, both of the Father and of Christ,

3 in whom are hidden all the treasures of wisdom and knowledge.

4 Now this I say lest anyone should deceive you with persuasive words.

5 For though I am absent in the flesh, yet I am with you in spirit, rejoicing to see your good order and the steadfastness of your faith in Christ.

6 As you therefore have received Christ Jesus the Lord, so walk in Him,

7 rooted and built up in Him and established in the faith, as you have been taught, abounding in it with thanksgiving.

8 Beware lest anyone cheat you through philosophy and empty deceit, according to the tradition of men, according to the basic principles of the world, and not according to Christ.

9 For in Him dwells all the fullness of the Godhead bodily;

10 and you are complete in Him, who is the head of all principality and power.

Out of God's Word...

Even though there is a chapter break in our Bibles, the final thought in Colossians chapter 1 is carried forward by the word "for" in Colossians 2:1.

1. *Paul's heart*—What word in 1:29 might complement Paul's use of the phrase "great conflict" in 2:1?

   How many different groups does Paul include in his concern (2:1)?

   What three things does Paul say (pray) that would encourage their hearts (2:2)?

   —

   —

   —

   Who are the two parts to the mystery of God (2:2)?

   How is Christ described (verse 3)?

2. *Paul's praise*—Not all is doom and gloom. Paul is greatly encouraged by the maturity of the Colossians. What does he praise them for in verse 5?

   And in verses 6-7?

3. *Paul's warning*—But the reports of heretical teachers and teaching are giving the apostle cause for concern. What are the words of warning found in verse 4?

And verse 8?

What is this false teaching based on?

—

—

What is it not based on?

4. *Paul's focus*—Paul has repeatedly mentioned Christ as the defense against this false teaching. List Paul's description of Christ in all His glory to this point:

1:15—

1:16—

1:17—

1:18—

2:3—

2:9—

2:10—

...and into Your Heart

- *Encouraging your heart*—Read 2:1-3 again. Your heart is the focal point of feeling and faith as well as the prime source of words and actions. When your heart is united in love with other believers and is maturing spiritually, you will have the ability to distinguish the truth from error. Look again in the previous section at "Paul's focus." How do these attributes of Christ encourage your heart today?

- *Mining God's treasure*—Read 2:2-3 again. Paul has already explained that the mystery that has been hidden is none other than Christ living in believers, whether Jew or Gentile (1:27). Now Paul desires that his readers gain a deeper knowledge of the things of God—a mystery that is not beyond reach. But accessing this hidden treasure of wisdom and knowledge will take ongoing effort. How much effort are you presently expending to receive God's available treasure? And what additional efforts must you take?

- *Continue to live in Christ*—Paul calls our ongoing relationship with Christ a "walk" (verse 6). Look up the following verses and jot down how this union with Christ is to be lived out in your daily life.

    Colossians 1:10—

    Colossians 4:5—

    Romans 6:4—

    Romans 8:1,4—

    Ephesians 2:10—

    Paul describes this vital union with Christ as being *rooted* in Christ like a plant, or *built up* like the stones of a building, or *"established* in the faith" (verse 7). With these same terms in mind, note a few changes that need to take place in your walk with Christ.

- *Your sufficiency in Christ*—Read verse 4 again. Then read verses 8-10. In verse 8, Paul restates his warning of verse 4 in a slightly different way. He warns we should not get carried away by any teaching that takes our focus away from Christ. He will supply all our needs, for in Him resides the fullness of the Godhead, and He is the supreme ruler of all. What more can you do to ensure that you keep your eyes focused on Christ?

Heart Response

Can you remember back to your life before Christ and its hopelessness? Paul describes that period of your life as the "power of darkness" (1:13). I know you would agree that it was truly the worst. You were a slave to Satan and his worldly lies. But praise God, He delivered you! He brought you to the light and placed you into the kingdom of His Son. So I ask you, why would you ever want to return to the same foolish, man-made, satanic lies? Stay alert! Be on guard! Don't allow yourself to be tricked by the lure of Satan. Keep your focus on Christ. Keep basking in the light of His grace. He is all you will ever need. And He has already proven His power in saving you. Allow Him to show His power by letting Him lead you through life. As Paul counseled, walk in Him and with Him.

Lesson 9

Describing the New Life

Colossians 2:11-15

*B*eing a grandparent is an incredible experience. Jim and I have had the privilege of being on hand for, or arriving within a day of, the births of all eight of our grandchildren. Enjoying the privilege of holding these new little ones and experiencing new life is such an astonishing experience. The miracle of physical birth never ceases to amaze us! But an even greater miracle is new life in Jesus Christ. Physical life starts at conception, but the miracle of a "new birth" requires being revived from spiritual death. Follow along as Paul describes what happens when, by God's grace, a person becomes alive in Christ.

Colossians 2:11-15

[11] In Him you were also circumcised with the circumcision made without hands, by putting off the body

63

of the sins of the flesh, by the circumcision of Christ,

12 buried with Him in baptism, in which you also were raised with Him through faith in the working of God, who raised Him from the dead.

13 And you, being dead in your trespasses and the uncircumcision of your flesh, He has made alive together with Him, having forgiven you all trespasses,

14 having wiped out the handwriting of requirements that was against us, which was contrary to us. And He has taken it out of the way, having nailed it to the cross.

15 Having disarmed principalities and powers, He made a public spectacle of them, triumphing over them in it.

Out of God's Word...

1. In verse 11 Paul continues his focus on the supremacy of Christ, which began in 2:5. To review, read again verses 5-10 and describe your relationship with Christ.

   Verse 5—_____ "in Christ"

   Verse 6—_____ and _____ "in Him"

   Verse 10—_____ "in Him"

2. Now starting in verse 10, continue to detail your relationship with Christ.

Verse 11—"in him" you were _____ with the

_____ made without hands

Verse 12—_____ "with Him in baptism," and

_____ "with Him through faith"

Verse 13—He has made _____ together

"with Him," having forgiven _____

3. Describe what's involved when a person is forgiven (verse 13).

   How much of sin is forgiven?

   What is "wiped out" or "erased" (NIV) and why (verse 14)?

   To where were these "legal demands" (NIV) against us taken (verse 14)?

4. Forgiveness also involves our being rescued from the domain of darkness. Why should you no longer fear the hosts of evil (verse 15)?

...and into Your Heart

- *Your new life illustrated*—Read 2:11-12. Paul is beginning to address some of his concerns regarding false teachers. These teachers taught that Gentile believers needed to conform to Jewish rituals and practices. So Paul tells the Colossians that, unlike the Jewish practice of *physical* circumcision, theirs was a *spiritual* happening. And that their baptism at conversion was a spiritual identification with their Savior's death and resurrection. They didn't need a false heresy filled with rituals and practices. All they needed was Christ. He made them complete (2:10). Baptism is a great illustration of what happens when we go from the old life to the new. Your old sinful life is dead and buried, and you have been raised with Christ to newness of life. Describe a recent action that showed you have "new life" in Christ.

- *Your new life initiated*—Read verse 13. The Colossians were once spiritually dead not because they hadn't been initiated into the Jewish religion with its rituals, but because of their sinful nature—*their flesh*. How does Paul describe this sinful nature in Ephesians 2:1-4?

    Dead in _____ and _____

    Who was our master (verse 2)?

    How did we conduct ourselves (verse 3)?

What in the nature of God spared us from wrath (verse 4)?

Read Colossians 2:13. What happens when a guilty sinner is made alive in Christ?

Christ's death on our behalf allows a holy Judge, God, to forgive those who by faith put their trust in Christ. How do these verses describe the results of this forgiveness?

Colossians 1:14—

Colossians 1:21-22—

Romans 3:24—

Romans 5:1—

Before believing in Christ, your nature was evil. Even on your best day it was impossible to please the holy nature of God. But with Christ you are initiated into a new life with a new nature. You are no longer under the power of sin. You are free in Christ! Can you think of a recent instance that proved your new nature, an instance that made you realize Christ's power in your life? Jot down a few of the facts here...and, of course, thank God for new life in Christ.

• *Your new life confirmed*—Read verse 14. You can enjoy your new life because you have joined Christ in His death and resurrection. When a person was crucified, it was the Roman custom to nail a list of that person's crimes above him on the cross. Read John 19:17-22. What was Jesus' crime?

Christ confirmed your forgiveness by canceling the written record against you by taking your list of sins with Him to the cross. Your debt is paid in full! Share several ways you could respond to this freedom.

• *Your new life protected*—Read verse 15. Not only did Christ's death on the cross pay your debt to God, His death also meant His triumph over "principalities and powers." The forces of evil no longer have any power over you as a believer because Christ has disarmed them. Describe again what happened, according to Colossians 1:13.

How does Peter describe what happened with Christ's triumph at the cross in 1 Peter 3:18?

Christ's present victory over the spiritual forces of darkness is assurance of an ultimate victory at some point in the future. With the victory assured, how should you view the future? Are there any attitude adjustments you need to make?

Heart Response

Take a look around. Many people are searching for life and meaning, but without Christ they will never truly experience real life, life in Christ. They are spiritually dead. They have a God-shaped vacuum within that longs to be filled, and they are searching for satisfaction in all the wrong places. Without life in Christ, people drift through their days and years with a sense of hopelessness. But praise God—when Christ comes into your life, He fills that void and turns death into life. Life has new meaning. You are fulfilled! And furthermore, your new life has limitless possibilities. God has taken up residence in your heart and mind. You are a new person. Old things have passed away (2 Corinthians 5:17). So live out your new life with all its potential.

- Live with more love—the love of Christ controls you (2 Corinthians 5:14).

- Live with more joy—the joy of the Lord is your strength (Nehemiah 8:10).

- Live with more generosity—give liberally (2 Corinthians 9:7).

- Live with more trust—God will supply all your needs according to His riches in glory (Philippians 4:19).

- Live with more strength—I can do all things through Christ (Philippians 4:13).

- Live with more resolve—in Him is your "yes" and "amen" (2 Corinthians 1:20).

Lesson 10

Staying Connected to Divine Power

*R*ecently Jim and I began preparing for a trip that would last several weeks. We have made these extended trips before, so there are certain things we do as part of the routine of getting ready. One of the most important tasks Jim does is plug in a portable battery charger in case our car won't start after several weeks in the long-term airport parking lot. When I walked into the garage I noticed the charger wasn't on, so I asked Jim about that. He reassured me that he had plugged the power cord into the charger, but upon further examination, we discovered the power cord had been plugged into the charger, but it wasn't plugged into the wall socket. Because the charger wasn't getting electrical power, it wasn't charging, and therefore, it was of no value.

Your Christian life is a lot like our battery charger—when you're not connected to Jesus, the power source, you will lack the power to live a victorious Christian life.

Colossians 2:16-23

16 So let no one judge you in food or in drink, or regarding a festival or a new moon or sabbaths,

17 which are a shadow of things to come, but the substance is of Christ.

18 Let no one cheat you of your reward, taking delight in false humility and worship of angels, intruding into those things which he has not seen, vainly puffed up by his fleshly mind,

19 and not holding fast to the Head, from whom all the body, nourished and knit together by joints and ligaments, grows with the increase that is from God.

20 Therefore, if you died with Christ from the basic principles of the world, why, as though living in the world, do you subject yourselves to regulations—

21 "Do not touch, do not taste, do not handle,"

22 which all concern things which perish with the using—according to the commandments and doctrines of men?

23 These things indeed have an appearance of wisdom in self-imposed religion, false humility, and neglect of the body, but are of no value against the indulgence of the flesh.

Out of God's Word...

Paul is reaching the climax of his argument, in which he exhorts his readers not to be seduced by man-made doctrines that have no spiritual value.

1. Review again Paul's concerns. Note his caution in verse 2:4.

   Then, how does Paul describe that which might "cheat" the Colossians in 2:8?

2. Christ won a decisive victory at the cross (verse 15). What does Paul tell his readers not to be fearful of (2:16)?

3. Rather than condemn these practices, Paul describes them as _____ of things to come (verse 17). Who is the thing to come (verse 17)?

4. How does Paul describe those who would "cheat" ("disqualify" NIV) or lure a believer away from the blessings that God intended (verse 18)?

5. What is the basic problem of these false teachers (verse 19)?

What does being joined to the "Head" ultimately produce?

This growth is not fleshly or worldly, but from whom?

6. Paul then addresses the problem of submitting to austere religious practices to produce holiness (verses 20-23). What is Paul's question to his readers (verse 20)?

What's involved in these regulations (verse 21)?

How profitable are these man-made regulations (verse 22)?

What two activities are involved in this self-imposed religious system (verse 23)?

What value do these practices offer for holy living (verse 23)?

...and into Your Heart

- *Focusing on Christ* (verses 16-17)—A shadow has no value apart from the object it represents. Paul told the Colossians not to let anyone tell them that the Jewish law and its practices had any significance apart from their connection with Christ, who was the ultimate fulfilment of the law. How does Paul explain the relationship between Christ, you, and the law in these verses?

    Romans 3:27-28—

    Romans 7:4—

    Romans 10:4—

    Galatians 3:24—

    Romans 3:31—

- *Focusing on God's prize* (verses 18-19)—Paul warns the Colossians not to allow the false teachers—with their false humility—to introduce teachings that divert them away from Christ and His grace. This diversion cheats them of their blessings as they become involved in a "works system" rather than in God's "grace system." How do these verses explain what Paul meant when he talked about a reward or price?

1 Corinthians 3:10-15—

Philippians 3:14,20-21—

1 John 3:2-3—

False humility is self-centered, while true humility is God-centered. True humility comes when we focus on Christ and His grace in our lives. If you are experiencing any success in your personal life, your church ministry, or in your home life, who should receive the credit and why?

- *Trusting in God's plan* (verses 20-23)—A man-centered religious system says that to reach God, you must exert some amount of human works. Each man-centered religion determines the extent of those works. Only Christianity is God-centered. What's involved in true salvation according to these verses?

  Romans 3:23-24—

  Galatians 3:16—

  Ephesians 2:8-9—

God's plan is simple. Put your faith in Christ, and He will do the rest. Paul said any human effort is "of no value." No one can make it to God on their own efforts. If you have trusted in Christ, offer up a prayer of praise for His marvelous grace!

Heart Response

The picture Paul is trying to paint for you—and me—is that Christ is all you will ever need both for salvation and spiritual growth. Man-centered activity looks good and makes people feel better, at least for a while, but is of no value to God. The only thing that has value is your connection to Christ. Christ said, "Without Me you can do nothing" (John 15:5). When you are united with Christ and keep your focus on Him, His life and energy will empower you for dramatic spiritual growth!

How are you doing? Are you more mature today than you were yesterday, or last week, or last year? If you're not experiencing growth and victory, check your connection to Christ, the source of all power. Remember, the tighter the connection, the greater the growth. And if you're disconnected and have lost your momentum and direction, reconnect again to Jesus. Reconnection is only a prayer away. Do it now!

Lesson 11

Focusing Our
Affections on Heaven

Colossians 3:1-4

e live at the best time in the history of mankind. Health and prosperity are commonplace in many countries around the world. Oh, we all know of the exceptions, and many organizations are striving to help change that. But especially in Western countries, we are blessed with plenty. This is both good and bad. Good in that we have enough to eat, warm clothes in the winter, and places to live. That's the good part. But the downside is that our abundance nurtures worldliness. We begin to set our affections on all the "stuff" we own or use...or want. Our garages are full of such stuff. We even rent storage units to keep all the stuff we cannot fit into our garages! And would you believe the apostle Paul addressed this same issue in his letter to the Colossians?

Let's listen in to the advice Paul gives about where we should place our affections.

Colossians 3:1-4

1 If then you were raised with Christ, seek those things which are above, where Christ is, sitting at the right hand of God.

2 Set your mind on things above, not on things on the earth.

3 For you died, and your life is hidden with Christ in God.

4 When Christ who is our life appears, then you also will appear with Him in glory.

Out of God's Word...

The apostle Paul is very logical in his approach to writing to different churches and individuals. As in his other epistles, Paul lays a foundation of solid theological teaching in chapters 1 and 2. He also makes a point of exposing false teachers and their false teachings. Now in Colossians 3:1-4, Paul begins to transition to practical issues. The heretics he has just written about have set their affections on earthly things, like fame and fortune. By contrast, Paul points out that Christians need to focus elsewhere if they want to experience holy living.

1. Earlier, Paul reminded his readers that as believers, they identify with Christ in what two events?

Colossians 2:12—

Colossians 2:20—

As a result, the Colossians are to avoid the world and its practices. But, not wanting to leave them with only a negative word, Paul then turns to the positive.

2. What positive event does Paul say believers share with Christ (3:1)?

3. What two activities are we as believers to be involved in according to verses 1 and 2?

    —

    —

    What is the opposite choice (verse 2)?

    Just to make sure you didn't miss it, how is heaven described (verse 1)?

4. For what reasons should we have this heavenly perspective?

Verse 3—

Verse 4—

...and into Your Heart

Paul has turned a corner in his letter. Having laid the theological foundation for holy living in chapters 1 and 2, he now begins to describe how to live out that holy life. He starts with the words "If then." This is not to suggest doubt, but to affirm facts about the believers in Colosse.

• *The place of our affection* (3:1-2). What spiritual activities are involved in seeking the things above?

God knows the mind is the gateway to our heart. What is involved in setting your mind on things above (see Romans 12:2)?

What steps can you take to turn your affections more fully in the right direction—upward toward heaven?

• *The person of our affection* (3:3-4). What are the reasons for having a heavenly perspective according to verse 3?

Just as Christ is hidden from all but those who have eyes of faith, so your new spiritual life in Christ is also hidden from view. However, this does not mean you are to keep quiet about Christ and keep your true identity a secret. What did Jesus say in Matthew 5:16?

Read John 16:33. Here Jesus tells His disciples that in this world they would have tribulation. What assurance did He give when He said that (John 16:33)?

What is our hope as we pass through this world with its trials and afflictions according to Colossians 3:4?

What encouragement for the present and hope for the future can you gain by knowing that Christ is coming for you?

Heart Response

These four verses are packed with hope and encouragement! When you realize that, by God's grace, you are a new creation in Christ and you have died to the old life (2 Corinthians 5:17), your perspective and attitudes should change. But unfortunately the old self doesn't give up easily. That's why the Bible commands us to "seek" and "set." Your life is different in Christ, so you are to act like who you really are—a believer in Him. Jesus said, "Where your treasure is, there your heart will be also" (Matthew 6:21). By realizing that Christ is your life now, you can have a new attitude. Your affections are no longer horizontal (set on this world). They are vertical (set on things above). So whatever happens, know, believe, and trust that Christ is your life, both now as you move through your busy and trying days and when He reappears to take you home to glory!

Lesson 12

Putting Off the Old Life

Colossians 3:5-9

everal years ago I invited the college-age girls from my church for an evening of fellowship and some of my mother's famous chili. We had cats-and-dogs rain all day long. But because our house was high and dry, I didn't think about whether the girls could make it or not. About the time they were to arrive, I received a call. Their van was stuck in an overflowing creek near our house! Immediately Jim called a friend who had a winch on his truck, and they hurried to the swollen creek to pull out the van and the eight girls in it. When the girls arrived safely at the house, they were soaked to the bone. I had them come in and exchange their wet clothes for all the dry robes and pajamas I had. While their clothes were in the dryer, we sat around a roaring fire, drinking hot chocolate, eating chili, and thanking the Lord for His grace in keeping them safe from all the raging waters.

Well, the apostle Paul tells the Colossian believers to do the same thing. He asks them to put off their old habits and sins. In the next section, we'll discover what he says they are to put on.

Colossians 3:5-9

5 Therefore put to death your members which are on the earth: fornication, uncleanness, passion, evil desire, and covetousness, which is idolatry.

6 Because of these things the wrath of God is coming upon the sons of disobedience,

7 in which you yourselves once walked when you lived in them.

8 But now you yourselves are to put off all these: anger, wrath, malice, blasphemy, filthy language out of your mouth.

9 Do not lie to one another, since you have put off the old man with his deeds,

Out of God's Word...

Paul says you and I live in two worlds, the "now" and the "not yet"—the present and eternity. When you became a Christian, you died to the old life and the control of sin over your life, and experienced new life in Christ (3:3). That's a one-time transaction, with eternal consequences (which make up the "not yet"). But you also live in the "now," in the present. Therefore, you must moment by moment continue to deal with the latent effects of your old life. You must constantly "put to death" the temptation to sin that is a residual of the old life. And the good news is that you have the resources to deal with the "old man with his deeds."

1. What actions of your earthly body are you to "put to death" (verse 5)?

   List the first two outward sinful actions of sexual sin and briefly define each. You can use a dictionary if you like.

   —

   —

   Now list the three inward motivations to sin and write a brief definition of each.

   —

   —

   —

   How does Paul further define this last action?

2. What does Paul say is happening to those who continually practice these sins (verse 6)?

3. What does Paul say about the past life of the Colossians (verse 7)?

4. A change has taken place and the Colossians and all believers are to rid themselves of not only the sins listed in verse 5, but also six sins of the mouth (verses 8-9). List them and give a brief definition of each.

—

—

—

—

—

—

...and into Your Heart

The believers in Colosse had been saved out of a deeply perverse Greek and Roman culture, but they still lived in that culture. Paul has heard of their struggles not only with false teachers, but also with various temptations from their society. Paul uses the imagery of discarding soiled clothing to describe the actions the Colossians and you and I must take when dealing with and discarding the sinful practices of the past (3:5,8-9).

• *Dealing with those who still walk in disobedience* (3:5,8-9)

Reread these two lists. What is the outcome of those who still participate in these sins (verse 6)?

In other letters, Paul lists sins that were often part of his readers' past. Read through each list below and give the outcome of those who were unwilling to repent.

List the sins in Romans 1:29-31.

Outcome in Romans 2:8-9?

List the sins in 1 Corinthians 6:9-10.

Outcome in verse 10?

List the sins in Galatians 5:19-21.

Outcome in verse 21?

- *Discarding the practices of the past* (3:5,8-9)

  How have you seen your life change for the better? Or, put another way, how have you changed—grown spiritually—as you've sought to "put off" wrong behavior and "put on" godliness? Be sure to thank God for the grace to make these changes.

Heart Response

What a great God we have! Whatever your past, He has dealt with it (Psalm 103:12) in Jesus' death on the cross (Ephesians 2:13). God has provided His amazing grace. Now you have the responsibility of doing your part—putting off your past and living in newness of life!

Lesson 13

Putting On the New Life

Colossians 3:10-17

I'm sure you have heard the expression, "Clothes make the person." For centuries, clothes have given visible clues about a person's financial, social, and even religious affiliation. But today, in our increasingly casual society, it's more difficult to tell the social or financial status of people just by the clothes they wear. Several weeks ago when Jim and I were waiting to board a plane I noticed a rather "scruffy" gentleman who was also waiting for the same plane. I wondered just how he was able to afford a plane ticket.

Was I ever surprised when he boarded with the first-class passengers! That taught me a big lesson: Never judge a person by what he is wearing!

As Paul continues his teaching to his friends in Colosse, he again takes up the language of clothing. In Colossians 3:8 Paul told them (and us!) to dispose of the old life with all its verbal abuses in the same way that we would dispose of soiled clothes. Now he urges us to "put on" a fresh set of clothes that will properly reveal our new character in Christ.

Colossians 3:10-17

[10] and have put on the new man who is renewed in knowledge according to the image of Him who created him,

[11] where there is neither Greek nor Jew, circumcised nor uncircumcised, barbarian, Scythian, slave nor free, but Christ is all and in all.

[12] Therefore, as the elect of God, holy and beloved, put on tender mercies, kindness, humility, meekness, longsuffering;

[13] bearing with one another, and forgiving one another, if anyone has a complaint against another; even as Christ forgave you, so you also must do.

[14] But above all these things put on love, which is the bond of perfection.

[15] And let the peace of God rule in your hearts, to which also you were called in one body; and be thankful.

[16] Let the word of Christ dwell in you richly in all wisdom, teaching and admonishing one another in psalms and hymns and spiritual songs, singing with grace in your hearts to the Lord.

[17] And whatever you do in word or deed, do all in the name of the Lord Jesus, giving thanks to God the Father through Him.

Out of God's Word...

Paul has already established that if you are a Christian you are buried with Christ to the old life and raised with Him to newness of life (2:12). You have put off the old man (3:9).

1. What do these verses teach about the actions you have taken and can continue to take when dealing with the sins that stubbornly cling to your life?

   Romans 13:14—

   Galatians 3:27—

   Ephesians 4:24—

   Ephesians 6:11—

2. What does Paul say about the new man—or new person—according to the following verses in Colossians 3?

   Verse 10—Describe the new man.

   Verse 11—Is a Christian to exhibit any distinction? If not, why not?

   Verse 12—What are five godly attitudes a Christian should exhibit?

   —   —

   —   —

   —

Verse 13—What are two more practices the "new man" is to put on, and why?

—

—

Verse 14—What quality is very important for the new man to possess, and how is it described?

Verse 15—What two additional qualities of the new man are mentioned here?

—

—

Verse 16—To what extent is the Word of God to dwell in this new man?

How should the Word of Christ overflow to others (verse 16a)?

How should the Word of Christ affect us personally and spiritually (verse 16b)?

Verse 17—What should be our goal in our speech and actions, and with what attitudes?

......*and into Your Heart*

A Christian is to put on a new way of life. But this new self needs constant renewal in order to keep it victorious over sin. How does Paul express this idea of continual renewal in these verses?

2 Corinthian 4:16—

Romans 12:2—

Ephesians 4:23—

What is the goal of this renewal process according to Colossians 3:10?

What does Christlike character look like? Keep reading.

- *It acknowledges no distinctions* (verse 11). The Spirit-filled believer doesn't see any social or racial barriers in the church. All differences are overruled and transformed by God's grace and power through one's union in Christ. This union produces unity in the church. List one thing you have done or could do to promote greater unity in your church.

- *It has a heart of compassion* (verses 12-13). The word "elect" means "chosen of God." God's undeserving favor, His grace, has showed compassion and set apart those whom He has bestowed His love upon. Paul urges believers to pass on God's graciousness and compasison to others. And this attitude should endure even to the point of bearing with and forgiving others.

Choose one of the following attitudes that needs improvement and list one thing you'll do about it right away. Also, choose one attitude and share how someone else extended it to you.

A sympathetic attitude—

A gracious attitude—

A lowly attitude—

A gentle attitude—

A patient attitude—

A considerate attitude—

A forgiving attitude—

• *It has a heart of love* (verse 14). What did Paul say about love in 1 Corinthians 13:13?

Christlike character should have, as its overarching cover, the virtue of love. According to Colossians 3:14, what does love do for the body of Christ?

Love is not just a feeling. It is also an activity. How have you demonstrated Christ's love this past week? Is there someone you know who needs Christ's love today or this week? What actions will you take to express that love?

- *It has a heart of peace and thankfulness* (verse 15). The closer believers are to Christ and His likeness, the closer they are to each other. Is there someone you need to go to and "make peace" with so that unity is restored? Also, how can you begin to nurture a more thankful attitude? Be specific.

- *It has a joyful heart* (verse 16). When you let the Word of Christ dwell richly in your heart and mind, you will be able to teach and build up others. And you will possess a joyous and thankful heart.

What different elements does Paul convey in his similar thoughts in Ephesians 5:17-20?

Once again, where does a joyous heart come from according to Colossians 3:16?

For more joy, spend more time in God's Word. How can you make that happen this next week?

- *Its life has purpose* (verse 17). Write out verse 17 from your Bible. Memorize it this week and make its message a habit and your prayer.

Heart Response

Unfortunately, Christian character is not something that just happens. I know you wish it did. You must nurture and develop it. Character is won over a lifetime, but can be lost with one sinful act. Yes, the old man is gone, but there is still a battle being waged with your sinful flesh.

To live out Christian character, you and I must renew our hearts and our character inwardly day by day through prayer and the study of God's Word. As we embrace God's grace, focus ourselves on Christ, and walk by His Spirit, we will be able to do all in the name if the Lord Jesus.

Building a Christian Home

Colossians 3:18-21

*C*hristianity is not a religion, it's a relationship—a relationship with Jesus Christ. When we became Christians, Christ supplied us with the grace to carry out the commands given in Scripture. God's power is supplied as His grace flows through us by His Spirit. Besides His power, God also provides us with a true pattern for living that will not only honor Him, but will also bless others. Paul is now ready to explain how Colossians 3:17—"whatever you do in word or deed"—fleshes itself out in the most important of relationships, that of the family.

Colossians 3:18-21

[18] Wives, submit to your own husbands, as is fitting in the Lord.

¹⁹ Husbands, love your wives and do not be bitter toward them.

²⁰ Children, obey your parents in all things, for this is well pleasing to the Lord.

²¹ Fathers, do not provoke your children, lest they become discouraged.

Out of God's Word...

In the last lesson we saw what Christian character looks like. Now Paul turns to the practical application of those essential elements as they are lived out in interpersonal relations—starting with the family.

1. Review Colossians 3:17. If you are married, how should you approach your specific responsibility as a wife?

   Next look at Ephesians 5:21. What posture should every believer take, and not just a wife toward her husband?

2. What's a wife to do (Colossians 3:18)?

   What is the moral limit of this role?

3. What's a husband to do (verse 19a)?

   What illustration does Paul use in Ephesians 5:25 to describe a husband's responsibility?

What responsibility is added to the husband's duty (verse 19b)?

4. What's a child to do (verse 20)?

   To what extent should a child fulfill this role?

   What reason is given for this command?

5. What's a father (or mother) to do (verse 21)?

   What caution and reason is given for this?

   What additional caution is given in Ephesians 6:4, and for what reason?

...and into Your Heart

- *The wife's role*—The concept of "submission" is not unique to Colossians 3:18 or to the responsibility of a wife to a husband. What do these verses say about submission in general?

     1 Peter 2:13-14—

     Why? Verse 15—

1 Peter 2:18—

Why? Verse 19—

What does Ephesians 5:22 say about the manner in which a wife submits?

What does 1 Peter 3:1 add?

In the New Testament, the word "submit" is a combination of two words with a military background. It means "to line up, to get in order, to arrange, to rank beneath or under." If you are married, are there changes you need to make to better follow God's plan for you to submit to your husband? Note several here.

• *The husband's role*—A husband is to submit to God's instruction to love his wife. According to Ephesians 5:25, who is the example for the husband's love and to what extent?

In Colossians 3:19, what word of caution is given to husbands about their wives?

• *The child's role*—Scripture calls a child to obey in "all things" (Colossians 3:21). It's not the child's wishes but his or her position as a child that is addressed. Children are then told such obedience is "well pleasing to the

Lord." Can you think of several steps parents can take to help their children desire to obey? Jot them here.

What can parents do to help children understand what is "well pleasing to the Lord"?

- *The parent's role*—If a child is to give unquestioned obedience, then parents must be on their guard not to discourage the child with unreasonable demands, humiliate them in front of others, or fail to exhibit a heart of compassion and understanding. What additional caution is added from Ephesians 6:4?

What steps can you (and your husband, if he's involved) take to better nurture and instruct your children? Here's one to get you started on your list: Make sure you encourage and praise each child at least as often as you reprimand or correct. Now list a few of yours.

Heart Response

The family is a matter of the heart for women. Tears are shed and prayers are prayed as wives, mothers, and daughters seek to do their best for their loved ones.

The family is also the basic unit of society. That's why we can say societies rise or fall on the health of the family. In fact, a healthy Christian family makes a powerful statement to the community. Each member is vital not only in interpersonal relationships, but also as a means of evangelizing the outside world via daily activities in the community. My prayer is that you—as a woman, a wife, a mother, and a child to your parents—are seeing the importance of your different roles and responsibilities.

Yet you are not alone in your obligations and challenges. God's grace is sufficient! He also provides you with tremendous blessings and power to faithfully carry out your tasks. He is asking you to show love to each member of your family and to provide an example of Christlike behavior and character. And you can count on Him to give you the strength and wisdom to serve as God's instrument in your family. It's a partnership.

Lesson 15

Knowing Who's Boss

Colossians 3:22–4:1

*J*ust as husbands, wives, parents, and children have mutual and reciprocal responsibilities as the "new man," so do masters and servants. Paul admonished Christian masters to treat their servants with fairness and honesty. This was a new concept to Roman masters because they considered their slaves as things, and not people. Masters had almost total control over their slaves and could do with them whatever they pleased. Few non-Christian Roman masters ever thought of treating their slaves with fairness—from their perspective, slaves deserved nothing.

The gospel did not immediately do away with slavery, but it did call for a change in the relationship between slave and master.

Colossians 3:22—4:1

22 Bondservants, obey in all things your masters according to the flesh, not with eyeservice, as men-pleasers, but in sincerity of heart, fearing God.

23 And whatever you do, do it heartily, as to the Lord and not to men,

24 knowing that from the Lord you will receive the reward of the inheritance; for you serve the Lord Christ.

25 But he who does wrong will be repaid for what he has done, and there is no partiality.

COLOSSIANS 4

1 Masters, give your bondservants what is just and fair, knowing that you also have a Master in heaven.

Out of God's Word...

1. What's a servant to do (verse 22)?

To what extent?

With what attitude?

For what reason?

2. What's the principle for all we do (verse 23)?

What's the reason (24)?

What's the caution (25)?

3. What's a master to do (4:1)?

For what reason?

....*and into Your Heart*

- *God's work ethic is universal*—Slaves are a thing of the past, but the principles in Colossians 3:22–4:1 carry over to workers today. What does the apostle Peter say about a worker's attitude toward his or her employer (1 Peter 2:18)?

What about a worker's attitude toward a cruel or harsh employer (verse 18)?

Why should an employee put up with such behavior (verse 19)?

• *God's worker is the best*—Review the parallel passage of Ephesians 6:5-8. What additional concerns does Paul express for a slave's work habits?

Evaluate your own work ethic at home and at your job. Are there attitudes or actions you need to change, eliminate, or improve? List the steps you can take to do so.

• *God's employer is the best*—Review the parallel passage of Ephesians 6:9. How does this differ from Colossians 4:1?

(Just a note: "Do the same things" in Ephesians 6:9 means that masters should have the same concern for God's will and for their workers as the workers are expected to show toward God and them.)

Does God have you in the workplace as an owner, a boss, or a supervisor over others? How does knowing that you have a "boss" in heaven who is looking at your actions affect your role as a leader?

• *God's power for the workplace*—Look at Ephesians 5:18-20. What admonition does Paul give in relation to God's Spirit and living the victorious life at home or in the workplace? Now review Colossians 3:16. The outcome is the same, but what is different about this admonition?

Ephesians emphasizes being filled with the Spirit, while Colossians emphasizes being filled with the Word. But the results are the same for both: How should walking by God's Spirit and being filled with God's Word affect your conduct at home or in the workplace?

Heart Response

In today's complex, competitive world, it is sometimes difficult for a Christian to obey God and hold his job or get a promotion. But regardless of the difficulties you may face, if this study finds you in the workplace, you are to obey God and trust in His grace in your situation. Unsaved fellow workers may take advantage of your kind heart and generous nature, but you can use your interactions as an opportunity to show the reality of Christ with your life. It is far more important for you to live for Christ than to make a few extra dollars. Remember, as you embrace God's grace, He will supply all your needs in Christ Jesus.

Lesson 16

Walking in Wisdom and Grace

Colossians 4:2-6

*P*rayer is a vital activity for followers of Christ. Prayer is how we commune with our God and Savior. We should not view prayer as some complicated or secret way of connecting with God. Prayer is simply talking with God as you would talk with another human. Because it's easy to explain and it sounds easy to do, you would think every Christian would have no problem talking with God—but that's not the case. If you asked even the most devout believers about their prayer life, they would probably admit to their need for improvement.

The apostle Paul has been describing how his readers are to conduct themselves "in word and deed" toward their family, work, and bosses. Believers are able to accomplish this because they have the gracious help of the Holy Spirit and God's holy Word. Now Paul mentions another resource God has provided for helping them to live out God's commands: They have prayer! In prayer, they can ask for God's grace and wisdom not only for their Christian relationships, but also for their outside relationships.

Colossians 4:2-6

² Continue earnestly in prayer, being vigilant in it with thanksgiving;

³ meanwhile praying also for us, that God would open to us a door for the word, to speak the mystery of Christ, for which I am also in chains,

⁴ that I may make it manifest, as I ought to speak.

⁵ Walk in wisdom toward those who are outside, redeeming the time.

⁶ Let your speech always be with grace, seasoned with salt, that you may know how you ought to answer each one.

Out of God's Word...

Paul evidently felt that what he was asking of his readers was difficult. Therefore he at once suggests prayer as a resource that would help assure them of victory.

1. *Paul's description of prayer*—Note here how Paul says we are to pray (verse 2).

2. *Paul's request for prayer*—What was Paul's twofold prayer request from his friends (verses 3-4)? Hint: Both requests begin with the word "that."

3. *Paul's exhortation*—What was Paul's fourfold desire for his friends (verses 5-6)?

Verse 5—

Verse 5—

Verse 6—Two elements of your speech:

—

—

Why were these two elements needed?

...and into Your Heart

• *An exhortation to prayer* (verse 2)—Paul, a man of prayer himself, reminds his readers of the importance of prayer. First he showed them the goal. Now he shows the path. That path is prayer. Husbands, wives, children, employers, employees, and all who would live out their roles in victory, are to "continue earnestly in prayer."

The constancy of prayer—Prayer is not just a habit to be maintained. It's a duty to fulfill. How often is it to be done?

With earnestness—This suggests a persistent holding fast and not letting go. How do these verses describe this persistence of prayer?

Romans 12:12—

Ephesians 6:18—

1 Thessalonians 5:17—

With vigilance—This simply means to stay alert while praying. It suggests the presence of danger—the danger of neglecting the practice or becoming distracted with the cares of this world. How did Jesus describe this vigilance to His disciples (Matthew 26:40-41)?

With thanksgiving—From your own experience, how is thanksgiving important in prayer, and how does it affect you?

How does Paul's description of prayer encourage you in your own prayer life?

(Note: How did Paul describe "the mystery of Christ" in Colossians 1:26-27?)

• *A strategy for prayer* (verses 3-4)—Knowing that prayer is a powerful resource, Paul goes on to ask for prayer on behalf of him and his companions. He doesn't ask for help to endure the hardships of prison life. Instead, Paul asks for prayer that he live as an effective witness. He prays for open doors and the wisdom and grace needed to share the faith.

Many treat prayer as an opportunity for airing complaints or even asking for some form of healing. Using Paul as a model, how can you change your focus so your prayers are more strategic?

• *A result of prayer* (verses 5-6)—Paul asks his readers to rekindle their need to pray in general, and to pray specifically for him as an evangelist. He also desires that they see themselves as ministers of the gospel as well.

Walking wisely with Christ—Wisdom is not limited to *knowing* the right thing, it extends to *doing* the right thing. Who is the source of wisdom according to Colossians 2:2-3?

How would a closer walk with Christ guide you in your witness with unbelievers?

Redeeming the time—Time is short. A Christian should make the most of every opportunity. Paul urges his readers to "make the most" of each encounter.

Considering your speech—Having embraced God's grace—His unmerited favor—should prepare you to share your faith with a spirit of humility. Also, living constantly in the sphere of God's grace should give you a winsome personality that makes the gospel message more palatable, in the same way that a seasoning like salt makes food more appetizing.

In light of verses 5-6, note several changes you need to make in your attitude toward sharing Christ with the lost, especially those outside your comfort zone. Then look to God and His grace to assist in making these changes.

Heart Response

Wisdom and grace are always needed for believers to be joyful and effective in their Christian walk. Relationships with family and other church members are never easy. And what about jobs and bosses and fellow workers and your next-door neighbor? These relationships also cry for wisdom and grace.

How can you and I cope with these relationships and give a positive testimony to the reality of Christ in us? I hope you picked up on Paul's clues. You are to immerse yourself in God's Word so that His Spirit empowers you to live as His child. And you are to depend on God's gracious guidance as you pray continually. These practices will ensure that God's wisdom and grace are available when you need them—whether at home, at work, or as you share and live out Christ to unbelievers all around you.

esson 17

Turning to Kindred Spirits in Christ

Colossians 4:7-9

o you have a longtime friend, maybe someone you've known since high school? Well if you have such a relationship, you probably know that person pretty well...and you may find it scary to think that person knows you quite well too! And if you're married, over the years you and your husband have probably developed a close and kindred spirit—to the point you're able to finish each other's thoughts.

I've often told women's ministries coordinators that if I get sick and can't speak, just have my husband, Jim, get up and speak in my place. Why? Because over the years we have developed a remarkable like-mindedness. Not only can we complete each other's thoughts, we can also complete each other's books if necessary!

As Paul begins to close his letter to the Colossians, he becomes very personal. He wants his readers to receive a firsthand report of his condition and situation. Because he can't visit them himself, he does the next best thing. He sends a faithful friend—one who knows Paul so well that he can accurately represent Paul to the believers in Colosse.

Colossians 4:7-9

7 Tychicus, a beloved brother, faithful minister, and fellow servant in the Lord, will tell you all the news about me.

8 I am sending him to you for this very purpose, that he may know your circumstances and comfort your hearts,

9 with Onesimus, a faithful and beloved brother, who is one of you. They will make known to you all things which are happening here.

Out of God's Word...

1. *God's messenger of grace*—How is Tychicus described in verse 7?

What was his twofold assignment (verses 7-8)?

What do the following scriptures also reveal about Tychicus?

Acts 20:4-6 (his roots)—

2 Timothy 4:12 (his ministry)—

Titus 3:12 (his ministry)—

What else do we know about Tychicus from Paul's letter to the Ephesians (6:21-22)?

2. *God's trophy of grace*—How does Paul describe Onesimus in Colossians 4:9?

Along with Tychicus, what was Onesimus' assignment (verse 9)?

List a few facts about Onesimus that are found in Philemon 10-16.

......and into Your Heart

- *Faithful in all things*—As you study the life and service of Tychicus, you find him faithfully going about his ministry as a messenger. Whether it's the letter to the Ephesians, or this letter to Colosse, or the letter to the

man Philemon, Tychicus can be counted on to fulfill his
assignment.

What goals does God set for His women in 1 Timothy
3:11?

Describe a recent task you were given to fulfill. How
would others evaluate the extent of your faithfulness?

• *Ministers of comfort*—What a switch! Paul is the one
in prison, possibly facing a death sentence. But what
is he doing? He's sending a delegation to comfort and
encourage his readers! What does Paul say about comfort in 2 Corinthians 1:3-7?

Who is the source of comfort (verse 3)?

What is the extent of that comfort (verse 4)?

What is the purpose of God's comfort (verse 5)?

What experience does Paul offer as an example of this
tremendous principle (verses 5-6)?

In what ways have you suffered that equips you to then
provide comfort to others?

• *Setting aside social distinctions*—It is noteworthy that
Paul uses the same phrase—"one of you"—to describe

both Onesimus, a runaway slave and social inferior, and Epaphras, a leader from the church at Colosse. Onesimus is God's trophy of transforming grace. He is a new creation (2 Corinthians 5:17) and Paul treats him not as an inferior, but as a "beloved brother." All former distinctions are gone. How should God's grace affect the way you look at others in your church or even in society?

Heart Response

Remember that close friend or spouse we talked about at the beginning of this lesson? Think about how your life has influenced that person. Hopefully, by God's grace, you've been a positive influence and encourager. The apostle Paul had just such an effect on Tychicus. So much so that Paul could send him out as his "clone." You too can have a positive influence—even on an unsaved husband or friend. And for sure, don't forget your children! Yes, they will learn from others, but make sure that what they absorb from you is a heart of love for them and a love for Christ.

Lesson 18

Acknowledging a Few
Heroes of the Faith

Colossians 4:10-14

ow many heroes do you know? Well, if you're thinking of the cultural heroes society tends to adore, such as A-list actors or professional athletes, your list is probably pretty short. But what if we defined a hero as anyone who simply has the courage to stand up for Christ, even under threat of persecution? Hopefully your list would be longer!

In the previous lesson, we began to read about the people who surrounded Paul. He was in prison awaiting trial, an enemy of the state. It would take great courage for someone to visit him and identify with him in his beliefs. To do this would be dangerous—guilt by association. And yet here they are, a group of men who were not afraid to be identified with Paul. Let's continue to look at this list of courageous men who were true heroes of the faith.

Colossians 4:10-14

¹⁰ Aristarchus my fellow prisoner greets you, with Mark the cousin of Barnabas (about whom you received instructions: if he comes to you, welcome him),

¹¹ and Jesus who is called Justus. These are my only fellow workers for the kingdom of God who are of the circumcision; they have proved to be a comfort to me.

¹² Epaphras, who is one of you, a bondservant of Christ, greets you, always laboring fervently for you in prayers, that you may stand perfect and complete in all the will of God.

¹³ For I bear him witness that he has a great zeal for you, and those who are in Laodicea, and those in Hierapolis.

¹⁴ Luke the beloved physician and Demas greet you.

Out of God's Word...

As Paul faithfully embraced God's grace, he (Paul) was like a magnet. Men of faith were at his side during every letter he wrote. Even in Rome, where his situation could test the most loyal of friendships, he could name half a dozen who were willing to lay down their lives for him.

1. *Greetings from three Jewish companions*—List and describe each on the next page (see verses 10-11):

Name of
each man   Description

—

—

—

What effect had these companions had on Paul in the past
(verse 11)?

(Note: There had been an almost total lack of response
from Paul's fellow Jews. The Jewish religious leaders had
rejected Paul's message and tried to kill him. They had
denounced him to the Romans, and as a Roman citizen,
Paul had to appeal to Caesar so he could get a fair trial.
Paul received great comfort from having these fellow Jews
by his side while facing trial.)

2. *Greetings from three Gentile friends*—First, look at what
   Paul wrote in verses 12-13.

   Note Paul's threefold description of Epaphras (verse 12).

   —

   —

   —

What was the goal of Epaphras' prayers?

How did this goal compare with Paul's goal for the Colossian believers according to 1:28?

Describe again Epaphras' spiritual efforts (verse 12).

How does that compare with Paul's efforts described in 1:29?

What is Paul's testimony of Epaphras (verse 13)?

What two things does Paul tell us about Luke in verse 14?

Who else offers his greeting (verse 14)?

....and into Your Heart

• *Two heroes from start to finish*—Aristarchus was a Jewish believer with a Greek name. Follow his history with Paul:

Where was he from (Acts 20:4)?

What happened in Ephesus (Acts 19:28-29)?

How loyal was Aristarchus (Acts 27:1-2)?

What further word does Paul give about Aristarchus in Philemon 24?

Luke remained with Paul through many of his trials on his third missionary journey. Where was he during Paul's final imprisonment (2 Timothy 4:11)?

How do these two men encourage and challenge you in your own faithfulness to Christ and to your church?

• *Two heroes with a question mark*—The first of these two heroes is Mark. What do we know of his past?

   Acts 12:25–13:5—

   Acts 15:36-39—

What seems to have happened (Colossians 4:10)?

What was Paul's final assessment of Mark (2 Timothy 4:11)?

What happened to Demas, and why (2 Timothy 4:10)?

Two men. Mark faltered but redeemed himself. And Demas started well, but faltered in the end. Jot down one or two lessons for your own life from these two men.

• *A hero thinks of others*—Did you notice three words Paul used to describe Epaphras' concern for the people back home? "Always laboring fervently." And Epaphras didn't offer up a quick, uncaring prayer. He sent up an agonizing plea of concern to God for the people in Colosse and for those in the other cities in the area.

With Epaphras' example in mind, how should you view prayer and the objects of your prayers?

Heart Response

This passage gives you and me much to think about. *First, there's the issue of courage.* God isn't asking you to die for your faith. He's asking you to, by His grace, live for your faith. Fortunately, for the most part we are not visibly persecuted for our faith, but the time may come when that will change. Allow these heroes to show you the way. Stand with Christ and His people. Be a hero!

Second, there's the issue of faithfulness. It's not where you start that counts. It's where you end that matters! Young Mark faltered, but by God's grace regained his footing and became a useful member of Paul's team. If you are one who has faltered, take heart in Mark's example. God can and wants to use you for His glory. Allow God's grace to dust you off and get you back in the race. Demas was another story. He got caught up in the world and abandoned Paul. Allow Demas to serve as a warning of the dangers of flirting with the world.

Finally, there's the issue of prayer. Don't think prayer is too passive to matter or make a difference. Become a prayer warrior who struggles for the needs of others. Also, pray strategically. Like Paul and Epaphras, pray for the spiritual growth and maturity of your family, friends, and the people at church. Pray often. Pray with passion. Pray fervently. Pray with faith!

Lesson 19

Being Faithful to God

Colossians 4:15-18

Over the years I have been involved in many small group Bible studies. These studies were challenging and helped me to grow and mature in faithfulness to God. Also, Jim and I have participated in small group ministries that were extensions of our church. These smaller groups gave us opportunities to use our gifts and develop friendships that have lasted over the years. A key advantage of small groups is that they create accountability among their members. As we end our study of Colossians, we see the dynamics of small groups at work in the house-churches of Colosse and Laodicea. Let's gain some insights into church life from its very inception.

Colossians 4:15-18

¹⁵ Greet the brethren who are in Laodicea, and Nymphas and the church that is in his house.

126

¹⁶ Now when this epistle is read among you, see that it is read also in the church of the Laodiceans, and that you likewise read the epistle from Laodicea.

¹⁷ And say to Archippus, "Take heed to the ministry which you have received in the Lord, that you may fulfill it."

¹⁸ This salutation by my own hand—Paul. Remember my chains. Grace be with you. Amen.

Out of God's Word...

From the beginnings of Christianity believers met in private homes. It wasn't until the middle of the third century that churches began to own property and build places of worship. Note some who opened their homes for worship:

Acts 16:40—

Romans 16:5—

Romans 16:23—

1 Corinthians 16:19—

Philemon 2—

1. *A fellowship between churches*—Read Paul's closing words to the Colossians in verses 15-16. What is the first thing Paul asks of the Colossians in verse 15?

What is the second request (verse 15)?

What two things were the Colossians to do with this letter (verse 16)?

What one thing were they to expect from the church at Laodicea and do (verse 16)?

2. *A charge to Archippus*—What exhortation did Paul give to Archippus (verse 17)?

3. *A personal greeting*—What did Paul ask of his readers in his closing remarks (verse 18)?

...and into Your Heart

- *The importance of the Word*—When Paul wrote this letter there were no New Testament books in widespread circulation. Most were still being written. So the churches were to faithfully copy and circulate the letters they received from Paul, Peter, James, and others. You can imagine how excited the church was to have a "first edition" Paul letter! Surely each letter was very precious to them. Therefore, they were eager to faithfully pass on these letters.

  How many Bibles do you have in your personal possession? How excited do you get about God's Word? In what ways does Paul's faithfulness to pass on the truths that are in the Bible affect your attitude about the importance of God's Word?

- *Finishing the task*—How easy it is to get sidetracked from serving God. Sin can put you on the shelf. Exhaustion can slow you down. Or you can just get mad and quit! It seems that Archippus was in danger of not finishing some task. Maybe he was to fill in while Epaphras was away, or maybe he was to take the lead in defending against an encroaching heresy. Whatever the case, Paul asked the church to come alongside him and encourage him to faithfully finish his task.

  How about you? Is there some unfinished task you need to complete? Or is there someone who needs your encouragement to stay faithful? What are some real steps you can take today to finish your task, and help someone else finish well?

- *A very personal greeting*—When Paul wanted to authenticate his letters, he often ended with a short note in his own handwriting. Share your thoughts about why Paul might have done this.

- *A prayer request*—Paul ends with a request for prayer—not for his sake, but for the sake of the gospel. He asks the Colossians to remember the reason for his chains. And he asks them to pray for his faithful preaching of the gospel, which had put him in prison in the first place. In what ways do you need to shift your prayers to focus less on yourself and more on others and the spread of the gospel?

Heart Response

Paul began his letter with "grace" (1:2), and he ends it with "grace" as well (4:18). He desires from start to finish that his readers continue to embrace God's unmerited favor. Ultimately, it is God's grace that strengthens and defends a church against heresy. Though false teachers might promise a deeper spiritual life through secret knowledge, Paul makes it clear that Christ alone is the source of spiritual life. He is the head of every body of believers, and He is Lord of both the physical and spiritual realms. I hope you've realized that true spirituality is not achieved through religious duties, special knowledge, or secret ceremonies. The path to a deeper spiritual life is through Christ alone. A truly wonderful and appropriate heart response would be to pray. Pray for faithfulness. Pray that you will never allow anything or anyone to come between you and your Savior, Jesus Christ.

Lesson 20

Greeting a Beloved Friend

A coincidence is defined as a remarkable concurrence of events or circumstances that weren't planned yet may, in some ways, be connected with each other. From a human perspective, the letter of Philemon describes a "coincidence."

A runaway slave named Onesimus, who is from a small town in Asia Minor, makes his way to Rome, hoping to get lost in the big city. Somehow he meets the apostle Paul and becomes a Christian, even though Paul was in prison at the time! And amazingly enough, Onesimus' master, Philemon, had also become a believer under Paul's ministry several years earlier—probably while Paul was in Ephesus, just a few miles from Colosse. Talk about a coincidence—or as we would say, the providence of God.

Now Paul writes a letter to his old friend, Philemon, who is in Colosse, asking him to forgive Onesimus, his runaway slave, and receive him back as a new brother in Christ.

Philemon 1-3

¹ Paul, a prisoner of Christ Jesus, and Timothy our brother, to Philemon our beloved friend and fellow laborer,

² to the beloved Apphia, Archippus our fellow soldier, and to the church in your house:

³ Grace to you and peace from God our Father and the Lord Jesus Christ.

Out of God's Word...

Paul usually dictates his letters, but because of the unusual nature of this situation, he decides to write this letter personally (verse 19).

1. *Paul's opening remarks* (verse 1)

   How does Paul describe himself?

   How does this description differ from the one given in Colossians 1:1?

   Normally Paul writes to churches about their problems and introduces himself as an apostle, which gives him the right to demand obedience to his requests. This letter, however, is not to a church, but to a person. From the onset, Paul wants his friend Philemon to know of his personal sacrifice in the Lord's work before he asks a sacrifice of Philemon.

See Colossians 1:1. What was the problem (hint: 2:4,8)?

What other associate is named in verse 1? How is he described?

Scan through lesson 1 and jot down some of the information about Timothy.

Having studied through Colossians, what is your opinion of Timothy as Paul's friend and fellow worker?

2. *Paul's greetings* (verses 1-3)

Who does Paul greet, and how are they described?

—

—

—

Who else is included in this greeting?

What two blessings does Paul offer to his friends in verse 3?

—

—

What is the source of these blessings?

...and into Your Heart

• *Paul's view of his situation*—This is the only letter Paul wrote in which he introduces himself as "a prisoner of Christ Jesus." How does he refer to this imprisonment later in the letter?

Verse 9—

Verse 10—

Verse 13—

Verse 23—

Paul saw himself not as a victim of the cruel oppression of the Roman government, but as one privileged to suffer for Christ. Here are a few questions for thought. How do you view your present situation? Do you see yourself as a victim who has to endure some horrible injustice? Do you complain to others about the unfair treatment you receive? Now for some answers: Who is the focus of this type of perspective? And how should you view each and every situation that comes into your life?

- *Paul's view of the church*—The church is not an organization. It's an organism. It's alive! It's made up of people, and Paul is quick to mention these people by name if he's had contact with them in any way.

  Philemon was a wealthy member of the Colossian church. He had slaves and a house big enough to welcome at least some of the believers in Colosse. Paul describes Philemon as one who works alongside him in the ministry.

  Apphia may have been Philemon's wife.

  Archippus could have been Philemon's son or a leader (fellow soldier) in the Colossian church, or in what other church according to Colossians 4:17?

- *Paul's gracious attitude*—Grace—God's grace, God's favor—is the theme of this study. God's grace to us should overflow as graciousness to others. As you continue through Philemon, note Paul's gracious attitude. He loved the church because he loved the people who made up the church. Was God's grace evident in your life this last week? Were you gracious to people during your last visit to church? What changes can you make in your attitude as you prepare for tomorrow and for church this next week?

Heart Response

The epistle of Philemon is such a gem! In a mere 25 verses, we glimpse an amazing view of the apostle Paul's heart. In this challenging letter, he expresses a gracious, loving attitude to a friend in Christ. His request is that Philemon extend God's grace of forgiveness to a slave who had run away from his duties. But before Paul makes a difficult request, he expresses profound love to Philemon, the recipient of his letter. There are many messages from Paul's heart to ours, aren't there? We have many lessons to take away from Paul, the master teacher and a loyal friend.

How's your heart? Have you forgiven any harm done to you by others? Ask God to fill your heart with abundant love, as He did for Paul and could do for Philemon.

Lesson 21

Nurturing a Heart of Thanksgiving

Philemon 4-7

oesn't it just wear you down to be around people who are negative or chronic complainers? It's almost like cantankerous people derive their purpose for living from seeing how many things they can find to murmur about. They take great joy in the number of people they can make miserable each day.

That definitely wasn't Paul's problem. He was just the opposite! In most of his letters he thanked God for something. He said, "In everything give thanks; for this is the will of God in Christ Jesus" (1 Thessalonian 5:18). Let's see how Paul expressed his thanksgiving in this passage.

137

Philemon 4-7

4 I thank my God, making mention of you always in my prayers,

5 hearing of your love and faith which you have toward the Lord Jesus and toward all the saints,

6 that the sharing of your faith may become effective by the acknowledgment of every good thing which is in you in Christ Jesus.

7 For we have great joy and consolation in your love, because the hearts of the saints have been refreshed by you, brother.

Out of God's Word...

1. *Paul's expression of thanksgiving*—What one word gives some idea of the kind of relationship Paul has with God (verse 4)?

   For whom is Paul giving thanks to God? (Hint: the word "you" is singular as it will be in most cases throughout the letter.)

   Paul had grateful memories of his time with many people. How does he express his love and thankfulness for the following people?

   The Colossians (1:4)—

The Ephesians (1:16)—

The Thessalonians:

1 Thessalonians 1:2—

2 Thessalonians 1:3—

2. *Paul is thankful for a faithful man*—What two things had Paul heard about Philemon's character (verse 5)?

His _____

His _____

Toward whom were these qualities directed?

—

—

Were there any exceptions to Philemon's love?

3. *Paul is thankful for a fruitful man*—Verse 5 describes the reason for Paul's thankfulness and why he is praying. But what is the content of his prayer (verse 6a)?

How can Philemon's faith become more effective?

What is the source?

What quality in Philemon gave Paul reason for joy (verse 7)?

What was the result of Philemon's actions?

...and into Your Heart...

- *Praying for others* (verse 4)—Praying for others was part of Paul's ministry. Remind yourself of some of what Paul had to say about prayer.

1 Thessalonians 5:17—

Colossians 1:3—

2 Timothy 1:3—

Paul's prayers flowed from a loving and grateful heart. Make a list of those nearest and dearest to you and pray, thanking God for them now. Note some ways you can make this a regular habit.

- *Living for others* (verse 5)—Paul had heard a report, probably from Epaphras, that Philemon had made no exception in his love and faithfulness to the believers in Colosse. The reason Philemon was able to live for others was because his first priority was to love and be faithful to Jesus. What is your reputation among the saints? What have you done recently to exhibit your love for others in your church?

What proof is there of your faithfulness?

- *Sharing with others* (verse 6)—Here Paul uses the Greek word *koinonia*, which means "fellowship," or speaks of relationships. Paul prayed that Philemon's faith would increase as he continued to interact with his fellow believers. There is no place for individualism in the body of Christ.

According to 1 Corinthians 12:7, why has God given us spiritual gifts? How have you been active and effective in sharing your love and resources with others recently?

- *Blessing others* (verse 7)—Paul's thanksgiving came from hearing of Philemon's aid to the saints. Hearing of Philemon's refreshment of the saints had refreshed Paul. Word of Philemon's ministry to others had traveled hundreds of miles to bless and encourage the incarcerated Paul!

Here's something to think about. What usually happens when others are around you? Are you a refreshing influence or do you drain others of their energy and motivation with complaints and problems? How can you have a more helpful and encouraging attitude that will, in turn, bless others rather than burden them?

Heart Response

What a delightful passage of Scripture! It's loaded with words of thanksgiving, love, joy, goodness, and refreshment. The heart of the apostle Paul rejoices and gives thanks to God. Why? Because he hears the news of Philemon's love and faithfulness. The news was like a cup of cool water in the midst of a dry and dusty land. In spite of his dismal surroundings, Paul had been refreshed by what he heard about Philemon's ministry.

As a result, everyone was blessed, including Paul. Make it a goal to nurture a thankful heart for all that God has done for you. Then faithfully demonstrate that gratitude to others through words and acts of kindness. Then others, in turn, can pass along this same thankfulness!

Lesson 22

Pleading for Forgiveness

Philemon 8-16

I've often heard my husband say that someone is an SNL, meaning a **S**trong **N**atural **L**eader. That would definitely define the great apostle Paul! He was a leader in the Jewish community before meeting Christ on the Damascus Road, and that character quality certainly became useful when he was commanded by God to serve as an ambassador to the Gentiles.

Paul needed to be a "take charge" kind of guy. As soon as he left a church he had planted, false teachers would come in and try to destroy his work. That's why Paul usually began his letters with the assertion of his authority as an apostle. In Colossians 1:1, we saw Paul use his official title to ensure that the Colossian believers listened to his concerns about what was happening in their midst. Now in Philemon, he picks up quill and parchment to write a personal letter to his good friend Philemon. Let's look at his approach.

Philemon 8-16

⁸ Therefore, though I might be very bold in Christ to command you what is fitting,

⁹ yet for love's sake I rather appeal to you—being such a one as Paul, the aged, and now also a prisoner of Jesus Christ—

¹⁰ I appeal to you for my son Onesimus, whom I have begotten while in my chains,

¹¹ who once was unprofitable to you, but now is profitable to you and to me.

¹² I am sending him back. You therefore receive him, that is, my own heart,

¹³ whom I wished to keep with me, that on your behalf he might minister to me in my chains for the gospel.

¹⁴ But without your consent I wanted to do nothing, that your good deed might not be by compulsion, as it were, but voluntary.

¹⁵ For perhaps he departed for a while for this purpose, that you might receive him forever,

¹⁶ no longer as a slave but more than a slave—a beloved brother, especially to me but how much more to you, both in the flesh and in the Lord.

Out of God's Word...

The opening "Therefore" refers back to verse 7 and gives the basis for the approach Paul is about to take in making his request to Philemon. What had Paul heard about Philemon (verse 7)?

Because of the love Philemon has shown toward the saints that Paul can make this request. Hopefully, Philemon's love will also include Onesimus!

1. *Paul's position*—Based on his authority, what action might Paul have taken (verse 8)?

   Paul's position was based on whose higher authority?

   (Just a note: in the Roman Empire, a master had complete control of his slaves. Under Roman law, Philemon had the right to kill his runaway slave, Onesimus, if he was caught and returned. This would make Paul's request a presumptuous one indeed.)

   How does Paul further describe himself (verse 9)?

   —

   —

2. *Onesimus' transformation*—Paul describes this runaway slave from two perspectives. First, what two things does verse 10 tell us about Onesimus' relationship to *Paul?*

   —

   —

   Then, what two things does verse 11 tell us about Onesimus' past and hopefully present relationship to *Philemon?*

   —

   —

3. *Paul's action*—What was Paul's decision (verse 12a)?

   (Another note: This action was demanded by Roman law. Maybe as Philemon is reading this letter, Onesimus is standing before him. Onesimus' willingness to return is evidence of his changed life and new nature [see Colossians 4:9].)

4. *Paul's reasoning*—Paul explains that his action is based on his personal interests. What are his interests (verses 12b-13)?

   What consideration does Paul give for Philemon's decision (verse 14)?

   What else does Paul say that might encourage Philemon to give Onesimus a favorable reception (verse 15)?

   What final personal note does Paul give about Onesimus (verse 16)?

…and into Your Heart

- *The power of God*—Paul uses a play on words in the original Greek text when he writes about Onesimus. He says Onesimus was not useful to Philemon, but now, as a transformed person, he is useful. The name Onesimus means "profitable" or "helpful." Formerly, Onesimus had not lived up to his name. He was unprofitable. But the grace of God through the gospel had changed all that.

As people look at your life, do they witness the power of God? List several ways you are useful to the body of Christ. What are some steps you can take to increase your profitability?

- *The process of forgiveness*—True forgiveness is a two-way street. First, the offending party, like Onesimus, must be truly repentant. This manifests itself in a changed life, which produces visible usefulness. But then there is the offended party, like Philemon, who must decide to receive the offending party back into his or her life. Are you in a similiar situation? Do you need to receive someone back? What will you do about it?

- *The providence of God*—Paul wasn't sure of what God was doing in this whole affair. He uses the word "perhaps" to speak tentatively of these events. But in regard to God's providential work in our lives, write out Romans 8:28 here.

What was Joseph's perspective in response to the cruel manner in which his brothers sold him into slavery in Egypt (Genesis 45:8)?

How do these concepts regarding God's providence (Romans 8:28 and Genesis 45:8) move you to more readily forgive others? Are you or a loved one facing a painful situation? How should you respond in light of God's providential care?

Heart Response

Forgiveness! It's truly a golden word to the hearts of sinners. And it's the message—and result—of the gospel. As believers in Christ, you and I are forgiven. What joy and relief this brings to our souls!

The Bible speaks often about forgiveness. It is a divine response to a wrong done. God forgives the repentant sinner. Jesus asked the Father to forgive those who were putting Him to death (Luke 23:34). And Stephen asked God to forgive those who were stoning him to death (Acts 7:60).

But what about forgiveness in personal relationships, with friends or family and in your marriage? In his letter to Philemon, Paul encourages us toward forgiveness. My friend, if you are offended, you need to forgive. Pray for the grace to forgive the person who offended you. And if you are the offending party, pray for the grace to repent—and hopefully be forgiven.

Lesson 23

Expecting the Best from Others

ou may have heard the saying, "Expect the best from others, and you will get it. Expect the least from others, and you'll probably get that too!"

Expecting the best of others is not always easy, is it? Usually, others disappoint us more than they encourage. As a result we become jaded and calloused in our view of others. And why not? We are setting ourselves up for heartache and pain. So, as a protection, we look at others with doubt, expecting the worst. But in this letter we are studying, Paul is expecting the best from his good friend Philemon.

149

Philemon 17-21

¹⁷ If then you count me as a partner, receive him as you would me.

¹⁸ But if he has wronged you or owes anything, put that on my account.

¹⁹ I, Paul, am writing with my own hand. I will repay—not to mention to you that you owe me even your own self besides.

²⁰ Yes, brother, let me have joy from you in the Lord; refresh my heart in the Lord.

²¹ Having confidence in your obedience, I write to you, knowing that you will do even more than I say.

Out of God's Word...

1. *Paul's long-delayed request*—Just before Paul makes his formal request, what inducement does he give (verse 17)?

   Up to now, Paul has commended Philemon's love and faith, and Onesimus' transformation. What request does he now finally make?

2. *Paul's offer*—Again, to remove any further doubts or hindrances that might be on Philemon's mind, what is Paul's offer (verse 18)?

   How does Paul prove the sincerity of his offer (verse 19)?

What does Paul ask Philemon to do with Onesimus's debt (verse 19)?

Then Paul reminds Philemon of what (verse 19)?

3. *Paul's benefit*—In the matter of accounts and debts, even if Onesimus' debt were fully repaid, what benefit would Philemon enjoy by responding to Paul's request (verse 20)?

Given Paul's dismal situation, it didn't take much to encourage him. He wrote to the church in Philippi, from this same place of incarceration, at about the same time he wrote Philemon. How would Paul respond to the Philippians' obedience (Philippians 2:2)?

4. *Paul's confidence*—What did Paul express confidence in (verse 21)?

How far did Paul's confidence extend?

(We don't know to what extent Philemon carried out Paul's wishes. From what Paul has already told us about Philemon, the outcome matters little, for whether Onesimus was allowed to go free or not, he would still experience the liberty of Christian fellowship.)

...and into Your Heart

- *Transforming the system*—Slavery has been a terrible blight on mankind since the beginning of recorded history. But amazingly, neither Jesus or Paul spoke out against it! What does Paul tell slaves to do in Ephesians 6:5-8?

What does Paul tell slaves in Colossians 3:22-23?

Paul doesn't directly ask Philemon to free Onesimus. He only asks Philemon to do the right thing based on the transformation that has taken place in his own life.

Reaping the consequence—Salvation means forgiveness, the wiping away of our sin. Onesimus had been forgiven by God and would hopefully be forgiven by Philemon. But Onesimus still had to face the consequence of sin. Did Onesimus steal from Philemon? Did Philemon have to buy a new slave to take the place of this runaway slave? Whatever the case, Onesimus had to suffer the consequence of his rebellion.

Is there a sin you are thinking about committing? Don't do it! There are always consequences! Someone—and you yourself—will always be hurt by any sin you commit. Look again at Eve's sin in Genesis 3.

What was the lure (verse 6)?

What was the consequence (verses 22-24)?

When you are tempted to sin, don't think about the temporary pleasure that might come from your sin. Instead, think about the hurtful and lasting consequence!

Heart Response

Paul definitely expected the best from fellow Christians. He assumed Philemon, his child in the faith, would act in the right way—the Christian way, the Christlike way. Paul had spoken of "putting on the new nature" in Colossians 3:12-17 with its resultant Christlike behavior. Because Philemon was one of God's transformed creatures (2 Corinthians 5:17), Paul could hope for the right actions on Philemon's part.

As God's child, you too are expected to act with Christlike behavior, in a Christlike way, in the Christian way. God requires the best from you. And to help you do your best, He has given you His Holy Spirit and His Word and all His grace. Draw on God's strength in times of temptation. When you do, He will respond to your obedience with joy—just as Paul said he would receive joy from Philemon's obedience.

Lesson 24

Extending God's Grace
Philemon 22-25

*P*aul begins and ends this short personal letter with a blessing of grace extended to his readers, including you and me. This letter is not just about an individual but an entire church in Colosse, and possibly also the church in Laodicea. In the opening of this letter, Paul asked for God's grace and peace for not only Philemon but also the entire church body. God's favor is offered to all through the saving grace of Jesus Christ, and this is where Paul begins. Because God's grace has been extended to Philemon, Paul asks Philemon to show that same grace to a rebellious, useless, runaway slave. Finally, Paul reverts to the entire congregation as he ends now with a prayer that all the believers would continue to experience God's favor in their spirits.

Philemon 22-25

²² But, meanwhile, also prepare a guest room for me, for I trust that through your prayers I shall be granted to you.

²³ Epaphras, my fellow prisoner in Christ Jesus, greets you,

²⁴ as do Mark, Aristarchus, Demas, Luke, my fellow laborers.

²⁵ The grace of our Lord Jesus Christ be with your spirit. Amen.

Out of God's Word...

1. *Making one final request*—What was Paul's last request (verse 22)?

   Why did he make this request?

   What was the basis for such a positive attitude?

2. *Greetings from five friends*—The list in verse 23 is identical to the list found in Paul's greeting in Colossians 4:10-17 except for which person?

   Review Lesson 18 and give a brief description of each of these men on the next page:

Epaphras—

Mark—

Aristarchus—

Demas—

Luke—

3. *Ending with a benediction*—How does Paul end the letter to the Colossians (4:18)? How does that benediction differ from Philemon 25?

....and into Your Heart

- *The place of hospitality*—The provision of lodging for itinerant preachers was very important in Paul's day. There weren't any Holiday Inns or Motel 6s. Christian travelers had no choice but to stay in a tavern or some other unsavory place unless someone opened their home. What do the following verses say about hospitality?

    Colossians 4:10—

    1 Timothy 3:2—

1 Timothy 5:9-10—

Titus 3:13—

3 John 5-8—

Christian hospitality may not be quite as necessary today because there are more options available to travelers, but it's still a desired quality. How are you at opening your home to others? How did you extend hospitality this past week or so?

• *A change of plans*—Several years before his imprisonment, Paul wrote to the believers in the church in Rome. What was Paul's initial plan, his Plan A (Romans 15:22-24)?

Obviously Paul's plans have changed. Now he tells Philemon he will travel east, not west. Do you have plans and goals? It's a good thing if you do. But how open are you to God changing your plans? How does Paul's plan of flexing to fulfill God's plan and God's will encourage you when your plans must change or are thwarted?

• *The place of grace*—What part does grace play in your salvation (Ephesians 2:8-9)?

In your spiritual growth (Acts 20:32)?

In relation to sin and the law (Romans 3:24)?

In missionary work (Acts 14:26)?

How does Paul describe the relationship between you, your spirit, and the Spirit of Christ in Romans 8:11-17?

How important is confession to ensure God's grace on your life (1 John 1:9)?

Heart Response

As you end this short letter, almost a note, you've probably been impressed by Paul's gentle and graceful spirit. Even the greatest of Christian leaders needs to take a lesson from Paul, who took his lesson from Jesus. Paul wrote in Philippians 2:3-4, "Let nothing be done through selfish ambition or conceit, but in lowliness of mind let each esteem others better than himself. Let this mind be in you which was also in Christ Jesus."

It's important to note Paul's gracious manner. He never forced his opinion on Philemon. His approach is a vivid demonstration of Christian courtesy and tactful consideration of others. It's especially impressive in our age of blunt and rude behavior even among believers. It provides a warm, personal example of the proof of the transforming power of Christ's Spirit—first in the life of Paul, and then in both of his converts, Philemon and Onesimus. Hopefully that transforming power is evident in you as well.

God intends that Paul's prayer for Philemon and the church that meets in his home should extend across the centuries to your heart as well. As then, and even now, may "the grace of our Lord Jesus Christ be with your spirit."

Lesson 25

Reflecting on God's Grace

*T*ake a few minutes to scan through each chapter of Colossians and Philemon, noting your personal thoughts regarding grace as it applies to your life.

COLOSSIANS

    Chapter 1—

    Chapter 2—

Chapter 3—

Chapter 4—

PHILEMON

Now, look through Colossians again, or through your lessons, and try to list at least five important facts about the person and work of Jesus. Maybe you'll find as many as ten!

1.

2.

3.

4.

5.

6.

7.

8.

9.

10.

Finally, note how each of these facts should apply to your life.

1.

2.

3.

4.

5.

6.

7.

8.

9.

10.

Throughout this study, I've been thinking of you and praying for you. My desire for you—and for me—has been that you will grow in your understanding and appreciation of the wonderful, matchless grace of Jesus. May we magnify His precious name forever!

Leading a Bible Study Discussion Group

What a privilege it is to lead a Bible study! And what joy and excitement await you as you delve into the Word of God and help others to discover its life-changing truths. If God has called you to lead a Bible study group, I know you'll be spending much time in prayer and planning and giving much thought to being an effective leader. I also know that taking the time to read through the following tips will help you to navigate the challenges of leading a Bible study discussion group and enjoying the effort and opportunity.

The Leader's Roles

As a Bible study group leader, you'll find your role changing back and forth from *expert* to *cheerleader* to *lover* to *referee* during the course of a session.

Since you're the leader, group members will look to you to be the *expert* guiding them through the material. So be well prepared. In fact, be over-prepared so that you know the material better than any group member does. Start your study early in the week and let its message simmer all week long. (You might even work several lessons ahead so that you have in mind the big picture and the overall direction of the study.) Be ready to share some additional gems that your group members wouldn't have discovered on their own. That extra insight from your study time—or that comment from a wise Bible teacher or scholar, that clever saying, that keen observation from another believer, and even an appropriate joke—adds an element of fun and keeps Bible study from becoming routine, monotonous, and dry.

Second, be ready to be the group's *cheerleader*. Your energy and enthusiasm for the task at hand can be contagious. It can also stimulate people to get more involved in their personal study as well as in the group discussion.

Third, be the *lover*, the one who shows a genuine concern for the members of the group. You're the one who will establish the atmosphere of the group. If you laugh and have fun, the group members will laugh and have fun. If you hug, they will hug. If you care, they will care. If you share, they will share. If you love, they will love. So pray every day to love the women God has placed in your group. Ask Him to show you how to love them with His love.

Finally, as the leader, you'll need to be the *referee* on occasion. That means making sure everyone has an equal opportunity to speak. That's easier to do when you operate under the assumption that every member of the group has something worthwhile to contribute. So, trusting that the Lord has taught each person during the week, act on that assumption.

Expert, cheerleader, lover, and referee—these four roles of the leader may make the task seem overwhelming. But that's not bad if it keeps you on your knees praying for your group.

A Good Start

Beginning on time, greeting people warmly, and opening in prayer gets the study off to a good start. Know what you want to have happen during your time together and make sure those things get done. That kind of order means comfort for those involved.

Establish a format and let the group members know what that format is. People appreciate being in a Bible study that focuses on the Bible. So keep the discussion on the topic and move the group through the questions. Tangents are often hard to avoid—and even harder to rein in. So be sure to focus on the answers to questions about the specific passage at hand. After all, the purpose of the group is Bible study!

Finally, as someone has accurately observed, "Personal growth is one of the by-products of any effective small group. This growth is achieved when people are recognized and accepted by others. The more friendliness, mutual trust, respect, and warmth exhibited, the more likely that the member will find pleasure in the group, and, too, the more likely she will work hard toward the accomplishment of the group's goals. The effective leader will strive to reinforce desirable traits" (source unknown).

A Dozen Helpful Tips

Here is a list of helpful suggestions for leading a Bible study discussion group:

1. Arrive early, ready to focus fully on others and give of yourself. If you have to do any last-minute preparation, review, re-grouping, or praying, do it in the car. Don't dash in, breathless, harried, late, still tweaking your plans.

2. Check out your meeting place in advance. Do you have everything you need—tables, enough chairs, a blackboard, hymnals if you plan to sing, coffee, etc.?

3. Greet each person warmly by name as she arrives. After all, you've been praying for these women all week long, so let each VIP know that you're glad she's arrived.

4. Use name tags for at least the first two or three weeks.

5. Start on time no matter what—even if only one person is there!

6. Develop a pleasant but firm opening statement. You might say, "This lesson was great! Let's get started so we

can enjoy all of it!" or "Let's pray before we begin our lesson."

7. Read the questions, but don't hesitate to reword them on occasion. Rather than reading an entire paragraph of instructions, for instance, you might say, "Question 1 asks us to list some ways that Christ displayed humility. Lisa, please share one way Christ displayed humility."

8. Summarize or paraphrase the answers given. Doing so will keep the discussion focused on the topic, eliminate digressions, help avoid or clear up any misunderstandings of the text, and keep each group member aware of what the others are saying.

9. Keep moving and don't add any of your own questions to the discussion time. It's important to get through the study guide questions. So if a cut-and-dried answer is called for, you don't need to comment with anything other than a "thank you." But when the question asks for an opinion or an application (for instance, "How can this truth help us in our marriages?" or "How do *you* find time for your quiet time?"), let all who want to contribute.

10. Affirm each person who contributes, especially if the contribution was very personal, painful to share, or a quiet person's rare statement. Make everyone who shares a hero by saying something like "Thank you for sharing that insight from your own life" or "We certainly appreciate what God has taught you. Thank you for letting us in on it."

11. Watch your watch, put a clock right in front of you, or consider using a timer. Pace the discussion so that you meet your cut-off time, especially if you want time to pray. Stop at the designated time even if you haven't finished the lesson. Remember that everyone has worked through the study once; you are simply going over it again.

12. End on time. You can only make friends with your group members by ending on time or even a little early! Besides, members of your group have the next item on their agenda to attend to—picking up children from the nursery, babysitter, or school; heading home to tend to matters there; running errands; getting to bed; or spending some time with their husbands. So let them out *on time!*

Five Common Problems

In any group, you can anticipate certain problems. Here are some common ones that can arise, along with helpful solutions:

1. *The incomplete lesson*—Right from the start, establish the policy that if someone has not done the lesson, it is best for her not to answer the questions. But do try to include her responses to questions that ask for opinions or experiences. Everyone can share some thoughts in reply to a question like, "Reflect on what you know about both athletic and spiritual training and then share what you consider to be the essential elements of training oneself in godliness."

2. *The gossip*—The Bible clearly states that gossiping is wrong, so you don't want to allow it in your group. Set a high and strict standard by saying, "I am not comfortable with this conversation," or "We [not *you*] are gossiping, ladies. Let's move on."

3. *The talkative member*—Here are three scenarios and some possible solutions for each.

   a. The problem talker may be talking because she has done her homework and is excited about something she has to share. She may also know more about the subject than the others and, if you cut her off, the rest of the group may suffer.

SOLUTION: Respond with a comment like: "Sarah, you are making very valuable contributions. Let's see if we can get some reactions from the others," or "I know Sarah can answer this. She's really done her homework. How about some of the rest of you?"

b. The talkative member may be talking because she has *not* done her homework and wants to contribute, but she has no boundaries.

SOLUTION: Establish at the first meeting that those who have not done the lesson do not contribute except on opinion or application questions. You may need to repeat this guideline at the beginning of each session.

c. The talkative member may want to be heard whether or not she has anything worthwhile to contribute.

SOLUTION: After subtle reminders, be more direct, saying, "Betty, I know you would like to share your ideas, but let's give others a chance. I'll call on you later."

4. *The quiet member*—Here are two scenarios and possible solutions.

a. The quiet member wants the floor but somehow can't get the chance to share.

SOLUTION: Clear the path for the quiet member by first watching for clues that she wants to speak (moving to the edge of her seat, looking as if she wants to speak, perhaps even starting to say something) and then saying, "Just a second. I think Chris wants to say something." Then, of course, make her a hero!

b. The quiet member simply doesn't want the floor.

SOLUTION: "Chris, what answer do you have on question 2?" or "Chris, what do you think about…?" Usually after a shy person has contributed a few times, she will become more confident and more ready to share. Your role is to provide an opportunity where there is *no* risk of a wrong answer. But occasionally a group member will tell you that she would rather not be called on. Honor her request, but from time to time ask her privately if she feels ready to contribute to the group discussions.

In fact, give all your group members the right to pass. During your first meeting, explain that any time a group member does not care to share an answer, she may simply say, "I pass." You'll want to repeat this policy at the beginning of every group session.

5. *The wrong answer*—Never tell a group member that she has given a wrong answer, but at the same time never let a wrong answer go by.

   SOLUTION: Either ask if someone else has a different answer or ask additional questions that will cause the right answer to emerge. As the women get closer to the right answer, say, "We're getting warmer! Keep thinking! We're almost there!"

Learning from Experience

Immediately after each Bible study session, evaluate the group discussion time using this checklist. You may also want a member of your group (or an assistant or trainee or outside observer) to evaluate you periodically.

May God strengthen—and encourage!—you as you assist others in the discovery of His many wonderful truths.

BIBLE STUDIES *for*

Books by Elizabeth George

- Beautiful in God's Eyes
- Breaking the Worry Habit…Forever
- Finding God's Path Through Your Trials
- Following God with All Your Heart
- Life Management for Busy Women
- Loving God with All Your Mind
- A Mom After God's Own Heart
- Quiet Confidence for a Woman's Heart
- The Remarkable Women of the Bible
- Small Changes for a Better Life
- Walking with the Women of the Bible
- A Wife After God's Own Heart
- Windows into the Word of God
- A Woman After God's Own Heart®
- A Woman After God's Own Heart® Deluxe Edition
- A Woman After God's Own Heart®—A Daily Devotional
- A Woman After God's Own Heart® Collection
- A Woman's Call to Prayer
- A Woman's High Calling
- A Woman's Walk with God
- A Young Woman After God's Own Heart
- A Young Woman After God's Own Heart—A Devotional
- A Young Woman's Call to Prayer
- A Young Woman's Guide to Making Right Choices
- A Young Woman's Walk with God

Study Guides

- Beautiful in God's Eyes Growth & Study Guide
- Finding God's Path Through Your Trials Growth & Study Guide
- Following God with All Your Heart Growth & Study Guide
- Life Management for Busy Women Growth & Study Guide
- Loving God with All Your Mind Growth & Study Guide
- A Mom After God's Own Heart Growth & Study Guide
- The Remarkable Women of the Bible Growth & Study Guide
- Small Changes for a Better Life Growth & Study Guide
- A Wife After God's Own Heart Growth & Study Guide
- A Woman After God's Own Heart® Growth & Study Guide
- A Woman's Call to Prayer Growth & Study Guide
- A Woman's High Calling Growth & Study Guide
- A Woman's Walk with God Growth & Study Guide

Children's Books

- A Girl After God's Own Heart
- God's Wisdom for Little Girls
- A Little Girl After God's Own Heart

Books by Jim & Elizabeth George

- God Loves His Precious Children
- God's Wisdom for Little Boys
- A Little Boy After God's Own Heart

Books by Jim George

- The Bare Bones Bible® Handbook
- The Bare Bones Bible® Handbook for Teens
- The Bare Bones Bible® Bios
- The Bare Bones Bible® Facts
- A Husband After God's Own Heart
- A Man After God's Own Heart
- The Remarkable Prayers of the Bible
- A Young Man After God's Own Heart

About the Author

Elizabeth George is a bestselling author who has more than 7 million books in print and is a popular speaker at Christian women's events. Her passion is to teach the Bible in a way that changes women's lives.

For information about Elizabeth's speaking ministry or to purchase her books visit her website:

www.ElizabethGeorge.com

Elizabeth George
PO Box 2879
Belfair, WA 98528